Departme
Scottish [
Welsh Office

NOTES FOR GUIDANCE AND LIBRARY OF STANDARD ITEM DESCRIPTIONS FOR THE PREPARATION OF BILLS OF QUANTITIES FOR ROAD AND BRIDGE WORKS

Her Majesty's Stationery Office
London

ISBN 0 11 550451 6

CONTENTS

PART A

Introduction

Conditions of Contract

1 The Conditions of Contract used for Road and Bridge Works contracts are the ICE Conditions of Contract, modified and amended as appropriate. One of the amendments required is the reference, in clause 57 and Appendix to the Form of Tender, to the Method of Measurement for Road and Bridge works (MMRB).

Method of Measurement

2 The MMRB has been drawn up to meet the particular requirements of highway construction and has been founded upon the assumption that full details of construction requirements are contained in the Drawings and Specification which have to be read together.
The MMRB has the following aims:
(a) To facilitate pricing by providing nationally standardised items.
(b) To provide a rational system of billing suitable for manual and computer operation.
(c) To simplify the measurement of work and the administration of contracts.
(d) To assist the financial control of the Works.
(e) To assist the retrieval of cost data and to improve the validity of cost data for use in the study of construction economics.

Specification

3 The MMRB has been based upon the 1976 edition of the Specification for Road and Bridge Works and the Standard Drawings, any amendments to either of the latter documents may require corresponding amendments to the MMRB.
The Specification for Road and Bridge Works includes such discretionary phrases as 'unless otherwise directed by the Engineer 'or' unless otherwise described in the Contract'. The intention is to give the Engineer power to act if the need arises. If this discretionary power has not been exercised prior to tender, then the item coverage will only cover the work described in the Specification.

Amendment to the MMRB

4 The provisions of the MMRB are subordinated by any express instructions to the contrary in the Bill of Quantities and for that reason any amended measurement provisions should in the generality of cases, be made within the Preamble to the Bill of Quantities.
In some cases the required amendment may be met by the use of a fully detailed item description.
In other cases it may be necessary to amend the units, measurement, itemisation and item coverage either collectively or individually and when drafting this type of amendment it is essential that the philosophy set out in the MMRB is followed and care taken to avoid reference to any matter which the Contractor is required to cover elsewhere in the Contract Documents. For these cases the amendments to the

MMRB are contained within the Preambles to the Bill of Quantities, such amendments being preceded by the wording given in the last Preamble to the MMRB.

Attention is drawn to Part C of this document which contains methods of measurement, notes for guidance and library of standard item descriptions for items of work which, whilst not being included in the 1976 Specification, are frequently required. Before they are used, the item coverages should be checked against the specification produced for the particular contract.

Where, through changing circumstances, any amendments to the MMRB are found to be consistently necessary and are felt to be of national application, then such amendments (other than amendments given in Part C hereof) should be forwarded to Quantity Surveying Branch, St Christopher House, London, for evaluation and possible incorporation into any standard amendments which may be issued.

Work Within and Below Non Tidal Open or Tidal Water

5 The requirement to measure work within and below water is applicable to all section of the MMRB. Whilst in the majority of cases the work measured as being within and below water will be readily identifiable from the Drawings, there may be cases where for clarity the limits of such measurement require to be delineated on the Drawing.

The words 'below the highest level shown in non-tidal water such as rivers, canals, lakes and the like' or 'below the highest level shown in tidal water' either as a subheading or at the end of the item description should be sufficient to enable the Contractor to price the works.

Computation of Quantities

6 The quantities to be entered in the Bill of Quantities should be those computed net from the Drawings. Any slight rounding off of figures shall be done so that the quantities represent as nearly as possible the work shown on the Drawings. Whole numbers are to be used except in the case of Steel Reinforcement, Structural Steelwork and Walings and Ties in which case the quantities should be to the nearest three decimal places.

Sub-division of Bills of Quantities

7 Bills of Quantities are to be sub-divided into separate sections in accordance with the first paragraph in Part III of the MMRB.

The sub-divisions given are typical for a contract containing work to only one type of road eg Motorway, Trunk Road or Principal Road. Where a contract covers work to more than one type of road then separate Bill of Quantities sections for Roadworks, Bridge Works, Accommodation Works and Works for Statutory Undertakers should be prepared for each type of road. Interchanges should be billed separately.

8 The levels of identification in the Bill of Quantities for Road works are :
Level 1 : Construction Headings
Level 2 : Section Headings in accordance with MMRB Part III paragraph 2.

The following table shows the Headings for Levels 1 and 2.

Construction Heading	Section Heading	Notes
Roadworks General	Site Clearance Hedges Fencing Earthworks	Safety Fencing to be kept under a Sub Heading.
Main Carriageway	Drainage and Service Ducts Sub-base and Roadbase Flexible Surfacing Concrete Pavement Kerbs and Footways	Foul Sewers, Lay-bys, Emergency Crossings, Police Observation Platforms and the like to be kept under separate Sub-Headings.
Interchanges	Sub-base and Roadbase Flexible Surfacing Concrete Pavement Kerbs and Footways	The main carriageway and drainage through the interchange should be billed under the Construction Heading Main Carriageway; bridges should be billed as Bridge Works (see paragraph 9).
Side Roads	Drainage and Service Ducts Sub-base and Roadbase Flexible Surfacing Concrete Pavement Kerbs and Footways	As for Main Carriageway.
Signs	Traffic Signs and Road Markings	Items of work for Lighting, Street Furniture or Communication Equipment including cabling should be billed under this Construction heading with an appropriate Section Heading or Sub-Heading.

Bridge Works Viaduct and other Structures

9 Particular attention is drawn to the extent of special back-fill requirements or embankment construction to structures. This work whether performed as a separate operation or simultaneously with the main earthworks operation should be shown on the Drawings and included in the structures Bills of Quantities together with any associated drainage work. The levels of identification in the Bills of Quantities for Bridge Works are either the name or number of each bridge, viaduct or other structure :

Level 1 : Construction Heading in accordance with MMRB Part III paragraph 3.
Level 2 : Section Headings which are generally the MMRB Section headings though in some cases eg Pile Tests these are Sub-section headings.

The following table shows the headings for levels 1 and 2.

Construction Heading	Section Heading	Notes
Special Preliminaries	Exceptional Temporary Works Interference Providing Access Excavation for Superstructure, and Dumpling Excavation Independent Checking of Erection Proposals	The section headings are examples of the type of work involved.
Special Foundations	Piling for Structures (including any Steel Sheet Piling shown on Drawings) Pile tests	Sheet-pile retaining walls should be billed under the construction heading 'Other Structure'.
Substructure—End Supports	Drainage and Service Ducts Earthworks Formwork for Structures Steel Reinforcement for Structures Concrete for Structures Steelwork for Structures Protection of Steelwork against Corrosion Movement Joints for Structures Waterproofing for Structures Brickwork for Structures Masonry for Structures Welding and Flame Cutting Procedure Trials	This includes skeleton abutments, bank seats, wing walls and any paved areas or treatment to side slopes. In the case of arched bridges this includes construction below springing level.
Substructure—Intermediate Supports Substructure—Intermediate Supports Main Span Substructure—Intermediate Supports Approach Spans	Drainage and Service Ducts Earthworks Formwork for Structures, Steel Reinforcement for Structures Concrete for Structures Steelwork for Structures Protection of Steel against Corrosion Movement Joints for Structures Waterproofing for Structures Brickwork for Structures Masonry for Structures Welding and Flame Cutting Procedure Trials	This includes piers, columns, trestles, inclined props, and their bases. In the case of arched bridges this includes construction below springing level.

Construction Heading	Section Heading	Notes
a. Superstructure b. Superstructure— Main Spain c. Superstructure— Approach Spans d. Superstructure— Arch Ribs	Drainage and Service Ducts Formwork for Structures Steel Reinforcement for Structures Concrete for Structures In situ Post tensioned Prestressing for Structures Steelwork for Structures Protection of Steelwork against Corrosion Bridge Bearings Movement Joints for Structures Brickwork for Structures Masonry for Structures Testing Precast Concrete Units for Structures Welding and Flame Cutting Procedure Trials Tests of Bearings	a. b and c. This includes deck superstructure and also framed structures which cannot be sub-divided into substructures and superstructure. d. This includes construction above springing level, spandrel supports and deck.
Other Structures	Drainage and Service Ducts Earthworks Kerbs and Footways Formwork for Structures Steel Reinforcement for Structures Concrete for Structures Steelwork for Structures Protection of Steelwork against Corrosion Waterproofing for Structures Movement Joints for Structures Brickwork for Structures Masonry for Structures Testing Pre-cast Concrete Units for Structures Welding and Flame Cutting Procedure Trials	This covers all miscellaneous structures such as retaining walls, subways, culverts of the pipe or box type which cannot be sub-divided into the other headings, corrugated metal structures and major river training works.
Finishings	Fencing Flexible Surfacing Concrete Pavement Kerbs and Footways Waterproofing for Structures Metal Parapets Brickwork for Structures Masonry for Structures	Road surfacing and foot- ways, kerbs, should normally be included in the B/Q for Roadworks; in the absence of such B/Q theses items should be included under this heading.

Construction Heading	Section Heading	Notes
Testing	Practical Tests of Concrete for Structures Grouting Trials Purchaser test on reinforcement after delivery	This is for testing of a general nature. Testing of a more specific nature eg Tests of Bearing are included in the Section Headings. Purchaser test on reinforcement after delivery should be covered by a Provisional sum.

PART B

Notes for Guidance and Library of Standard Item Descriptions

General

1 The library has been compiled in accordance with the itemisation features of the MMRB. This is a master library which can be used direct for manual billing, or as the basis from which individual libraries can be constructed to suit available computer facilities. Whatever process is followed the end result should produce directly comparable Bills of Quantities.

The root narratives contain lettered inserts which can, by the use of a numbered variable from the appropriate lettered group, produce unique item descriptions for all standard constructional work. For example, the information in the Specification or on the drawings may show the requirements for fencing as '1·3 metres high standard four rail motorway fence with stockproofing of a single strand of galvanised barbed wire.'

By referring to **Section 4: Fencing,** a unique item description can be built up as follows:

Root Narrative Item 2—*JB* motorway fence *G* high with ***CDET***

Variables

JO = no entry—no entry to be made against *J*

B2 = four rail—selected from Group *B*

G1 = 1·3 metres—unique height

C1 = one strand of galvanised barbed wire—selected from Group *C*

DO = no entry—no entry to be made against *D*

EO = no entry—no entry to be made against *E*

T1 = PR100100—Derived from Standard Drawings

Similarly, by referring to **Section 13: Piling,** a unique item description for piling requirements, which may be shown as, 'vertical 3·5 metre 600 mm cast in place piles' would be as follows:

Root Narrative Item 8—*DE* diameter cast-in-place pile shaft *N C A*

Variables

D1 = Vertical—selected from Group *D*

E7 = 600mm—selected from Group *E*

NO = no entry—no entry to be made against *N*

C1 = not exceeding 5 metres in length—selected from Group *C*

A2 = in main piling—selected from Group *A*

Amendments to the Library

2 Any variable not listed in a group but belonging to a group generically may be added to it and numbered sequentially. Items which cannot be compiled from the existing root narratives are rogue items and if required they should be drafted on the same principles as the Standard Item Library and inserted as necessary in the Bill of Quantities.

As in the case of the MMRB, rogues and additional variables not contained in the Item Library but which are found to be consistently necessary and are felt to be of national application should be forwarded to Quantity Surveying Branch, St Christopher House, London for evaluation and possible incorporation into any standard amendments which may be issued.

**Reference to
Specification Clauses**

3 Where a Specification Clause is quoted in the Notes this refers to the Clause Numbers contained in the 1976 Edition of the Specification for Road and Bridge Works.

Section 1: Preliminaries

Item	Root Narratives	Unit
	Temporary Accommodation	
1	*A* of principal offices for the Engineer.	Item
2	*A* of principal laboratories for the Engineer.	Item
3	*A* of portable offices for the Engineer.	Item
4	*A* of portable laboratories for the Engineer.	Item
5	*A* of offices and messes for the Contractor.	Item
6	*A* of stores and workshops for the Contractor.	Item
7	Servicing of principal offices for the Engineer *B*	Item
8	Servicing of portable offices for the Engineer *B*	Item
	Operatives for the Engineer	
9	Chainman/driver for the Engineer.	Day
10	Laboratory handyman/driver for the Engineer.	Day
	Traffic Safety and Control (Traffic Safety Measures)	
11	Traffic safety and control	Item
	Temporary Diversion of Traffic	
12	*C* temporary diversion of traffic at location *D* listed in the Schedule	Item
13	*C* temporary diversion of traffic at those locations listed in the Schedule but not measured individually.	Item
	Vehicles for the Engineer	
14	*E* for the Engineer.	Veh Wk
	Progress Photographs	
15	Set of progress photographs comprising *F* negatives plus *G H* prints from each negative	No
16	Set of aerial progress photographs comprising *F* negatives plus *G H* prints from each negative.	No
17	Additional progress photographs.	No
18	Additional aerial progress photographs.	No

Group	Variables		
A	*1*	=	Erection
	2	=	Servicing
	3	=	Dismantling

Group	Variables		
B	1	=	until completion of Works
	2	=	during the period up to the issue of the Maintenance Certificate
C	1	=	Taking measures for or construction of
	2	=	Maintenance of
	3	=	Removal of
D	1 etc =		[Engineers schedule reference number or letter]
E	1 etc =		[each type of vehicle]
F	1 etc =		[number of negatives]
G	1 etc =		[number of prints]
H	1	=	quarter plate
	2	=	half plate
	3	=	whole plate

Temporary Accommodation

Notes

1 The precise details of the Engineer's requirements for temporary accommodation in the form of offices and laboratories together with any equipment, furniture, fittings, supplies and consumable stores should be given by means of Drawings and/or Schedules which should also separately identify any items of equipment and the like which will become the property of the Employer.

The Drawings and/or Schedules should similarly identify the temporary accommodation required by the Engineer to remain for occupation and use, in accordance with Specification Clause 101.4, during the period up to the issue of the Maintenance Certificate. In cases where the temporary accommodation requires modifying at any time up to the issue of the Maintenance Certificate then the MMRB should be amended, as shown in Part C hereof, by means of a preamble to the Bill of Quantities.

Supplies are those items which will require maintaining during the currency of the Contract but which are capable of being returned to the Contractor when no longer required whilst consumable stores are those which only require replenishing such as soap, paper towels, toilet rolls and the like.

The charges for photo copying facilities vary considerably between companies in that some companies have inclusive charges for servicing, paper, chemicals and the like whilst others charge separately. Where the Engineer requires these facilities to be provided he should ascertain the relevant information required in order that the Contractor may cover for this facility in his rates and prices.

Traffic Safety and Control

2 Whilst the Schedule required by Specification Clause 103.2 may be amalgamated with that of Clause 104, locations pertaining to traffic safety and control should be separately identified in the amalgamated schedule. One item should be provided in the Bill of Quantities to cover for all such locations so identified.

Temporary Diversion of Traffic

3 Temporary Diversion of Traffic should be separately measured for those locations where the diversionary work involved is likely to be complicated, expensive, or where its impact or disruption on the Works is likely to be substantial and in these cases the item description should include the appropriate Schedule reference.

Diversions of a minor nature at locations listed in the Schedule should be billed as one item but the item description should include all the appropriate Schedule references.

Special Preliminaries

4 The preliminary items contained in this Section relate entirely to preliminaries applicable to the whole of the Works. 'Special Preliminaries' are more usual to Bridge Works although they may on occasions be required for Road Works. Their inclusion in Contracts is however entirely at the Engineer's discretion and should be limited to those preliminaries which, because of the magnitude of their cost for any one bridge or structure would unduly distort the rates and prices of the main construction items for that bridge or structure.

Examples of special preliminaries that may occur are given in the following paragraphs :—

(a) Exceptional Temporary Works

The Contractor is normally contractually bound to allow for temporary works in his rates and prices. When however, exceptional temporary works are specified which are likely to be expensive in relation to the permanent works, then additional items should be provided in the Bill of Quantities as appropriate thereby giving the tenderer the opportunity of separately pricing for such work in addition to his normal contractual obligations.

When such temporary works are itemised, this in no way changes the contractual position by which the Contractor is responsible for the adequacy stability and safety of temporary works, although the Engineer may prescribe particular minimum loading and clearance criteria where appropriate, eg for a temporary highway bridge. The nature of any requirement for exceptional temporary works and their extent should be fully described on the Drawings with, if necessary, an additional specification clause.

Circumstances occasionally arise in which works of a temporary nature are required to conform to an obligatory design prepared by the Engineer, who, because he designed them, will be responsible for their structural adequacy.

(b) Interference

Where some specific interference with the Works is foreseeable which is expected to have a significant effect upon the cost and progress of the work, an item should be provided for interference.

(c) Providing Access

Normally the provision of access to or through the sites of structures is covered by the general items for the Contract as a whole and nothing further is required. However, occasionally there may be cases where providing or maintaining access will be a substantial proportion of the total cost of a structure, or where the necessity for special access is related to the particular design of the structure. In such cases a special item would be appropriate.

(d) Excavation for Superstructure and Dumpling Excavation

Bulk excavation is measured under the 'Earthworks' section of the Bill and, since the adoption of dumpling excavation is normally a matter of Contractor's choice, no special measurement for this is included in the Earthworks section. If, however, this form of excavation is required by the Contract then an item to cover the extra cost of dumpling excavation should be included as a Special Preliminaries item in the Structure Bill. In such cases the Drawing should show the extent and requirements of the Engineer.

(e) Independent Checking of Erection Proposals

Technical Memorandum entitled 'The Independent Checking of Erection Proposals and Temporary Works Details for Major Highway Structures on Trunk Roads and Motorways' sets out the procedures to be adopted and the necessary amendments to be made to the Contract Documentation including the wording of a new clause numbered 8A for insertion in the ICE Conditions of Contract 5th Edition. As far as the BQ's are concerned this Tech Memo requires a priceable lump sum item to be inserted in the Special Preliminaries for each structure to which reference is made in Clause 8A. The wording of this item shall, in all cases, read:

Checking of erection proposals and/or temporary works details in accordance with supplementary clause 8A of the Conditions of Contract.

Section 2: Site Clearance

Item	Root Narratives	Unit
1	General Site Clearance.	hectare
2	General site clearance area *A*.	hectare
3	Demolition of building or structure reference No *B*	Item
4	Demolition of group of buildings or structures reference No *B*	Item
5	Removal of disused sewers or drains *C* diameter with 1 metre or less of cover to formation level.	lin m

Group	Variables	
A	*1* etc =	[Engineers letter reference]
B	*1* etc =	[Engineers reference]
C	*1* etc =	[diameter to be stated]

Notes

General Site Clearance
1 General site clearance (item 1) should only be used for those cases where the clearance of the whole site is not markedly different. Where sections of the site are different in character and therefore the clearance is markedly different then the whole site should be broken down into separate sections and each section measured under item 2.

Buildings and Structures
2 Each building or structure or group of buildings or structures to be demolished should be marked on the Site Clearance Drawings with a reference number and this should be included in the bill item. Any special requirements for demolition of buildings should be clearly described in the Contract. It should be appreciated that on drawings even of 1/500 scale, it is often difficult to determine precisely the extent of buildings and whether (in some cases) outbuildings are to be demolished. Sufficient descriptions should be included on the Drawings or in the Specification to define the extent of demolition required.

Disused Sewers and Drains
3 Disused sewers or drains with 1 metre or less of cover to formation level should always be shown on the Drawings and the diameter stated.

Section 3: Hedges

Item	Root Narratives	Unit
	Hedges	
1	*A* hedge with plants *B* apart *C*.	lin m
	Excavation in Rock and Reinforced Concrete	
2	Extra over any item of hedges for excavation in *D*	cu m

Group	Variables		
A	*1*	=	Quickthorn
	2	=	Privet
	3	=	Beech
	4	=	Holly
	5	=	Lawsons cypress
B	*1*	=	225mm
	2	=	300mm
	3	=	375mm
	4	=	450mm
	5	=	525mm
	6	=	600mm
	7	=	675mm
	8	=	750mm
	9	=	825mm
	10	=	1 metre
C	*0*	=	No entry
	1	=	with protective fence one side
	2	=	with protective fence both sides
D	*1*	=	rock
	2	=	reinforced concrete

Note

Hedges

1 The Drawings should indicate the position of hedge lines. The species of hedges and plant spacing should also be shown. Where necessary, requirements for protective fencing and for fertilising of the soil before planting should be indicated on the Drawings.

Section 4: Fencing

Item	Root Naratives	Unit
	Fences, Gates and Stiles	
1	Stated temporary fence *A*.	lin m
2	*J B* motorway fence *G* high with *C D E T*.	lin m
3	*J F* fence *G* high with *H C D E T*	lin m
4	*J* wooden post and *B* fence *G* high with *C D E T*	lin m
5	*J I K* gate *G* high *G* wide.	No
6	*I* stile *L*.	No
7	Removal and re-erection of existing *J B* motorway fence *G* high with *C D E T*	lin m
8	Removal and re-erection of existing *J F* fence *G* high with *H C D E*	lin m
9	Removal and re-erection of existing *J* wooden post and *B* fence *G* high with *C D E T*	lin m
10	Concrete footing to intermediate posts for *U* fence	No
11	Removal and re-erection of existing *J I K* gate *G* high *G* wide.	No
12	Removal and re-erection of existing *I* stile *L*	No
	Safety Fences	
13	Untensioned *N M*.	lin m
14	Tensioned *N M*.	lin m
15	Driven *O* post *P* for *N M*.	No
16	*O* post *P* for setting in concrete for *N M*.	No
17	*O* post *P* fixed to concrete for *N M*.	No
18	Mounting bracket *Q* fixed to structure for *N M*.	No
19	Terminal for untensioned *N M*.	No
20	Terminal for tensioned *N M*.	No
21	Full height anchorage for *N M*.	No
22	Expansion joint anchorage for *N M*.	No
23	*R* connection of *N M* to bridge parapet.	No
24	Transition piece for open box beam to *N* corrugated beam.	No
25	Concrete footing for *O* post for *M*.	No
26	Concrete footing spanning french drain for *O* post for *M R*.	No
27	Removal of existing safety fence.	lin m
	Excavation in Rock and Reinforced Concrete	
28	Extra over any item of fencing for excavation in *S*.	cu m

Group	Variables		
A	1	=	Type 1
	2	=	Type 2
	3	=	Type 3
	4	=	Type 4
	5	=	Type 4A
	6	=	[Engineers Type reference]
B	1	=	three rail
	2	=	four rail
	3	=	five rail
C	0	=	No entry
	1	=	one strand of galvanised barbed wire
	2	=	two strands of galvanised barbed wire
	3	=	three strands of galvanised barbed wire
	4	=	one strand galvanised plastic coated barbed wire
	5	=	two strands galvanised plastic coated barbed wire
	6	=	three strands galvanised plastic coated barbed wire
	7	=	one strand galvanised bonded plastic coated barbed wire
	8	=	two strands galvanised bonded plastic coated barbed wire
	9	=	three strands galvanised bonded plastic coated barbed wire
D	0	=	No entry
	1	=	one strand of galvanised plain wire
	2	=	two strands of galvanised plain wire
	3	=	three strands of galvanised plain wire
	4	=	one strand galvanised plastic coated plain wire
	5	=	two strands galvanised plastic coated plain wire
	6	=	three strands galvanised plastic coated plain wire
	7	=	one strand galvanised bonded plastic coated plain wire
	8	=	two strands galvanised bonded plastic coated plain wire
	9	=	three strands galvanised bonded plastic coated plain wire
E	0	=	No entry
	1	=	galvanised pig netting
	2	=	bonded plastic coated pig netting
	3	=	galvanised sheep netting
	4	=	galvanised large hexagon, sheep netting
	5	=	galvanised small hexagon chicken netting
	6	=	galvanised chain link
	7	=	plastic coated chain link
F	1	=	plastic coated chain link

Group	Variables		
F contd.	**2**	=	galvanised chain link
	3	=	cleft chestnut pale
	4	=	mild steel bar
	5	=	wrought iron bar
	6	=	woven wire
	7	=	strained wire
	8	=	close boarded
	9	=	wood palisade
	10	=	woven wood
G	**1** etc =		[Unique height for fences; unique height and width for gates as required]
H	**1**	=	concrete posts
	2	=	concrete posts with cranked top
	3	=	concrete posts with bonded plastic coated extension arm
	4	=	wooden posts
	5	=	wooden posts with bonded plastic coated extension arms
	6	=	steel angle posts
	7	=	steel angle posts with cranked top
	8	=	steel angle posts with extension arm
	9	=	bonded plastic coated steel RHS post
	10	=	bonded plastic coated steel RHS post with cranked top
	11	=	bonded plastic coated steel RHS post with extension arm
	12	=	bonded plastic coated steel pylon post
	13	=	steel standard and pillars
	14	=	cast iron posts
	15	=	wrought iron posts
	16	=	mild steel posts
I	**1**	=	steel tubular frame
	2	=	timber
J	**0**	=	No entry
	1	=	Painted
K	**1**	=	single field
	2	=	half mesh single field
	3	=	extra wide single field
	4	=	double field
	5	=	Type 1 wicket
	6	=	Type 2 wicket
	7	=	kissing
	8	=	Type [Engineers reference]

Group	Variables		
L	1	=	Type 1
	2	=	Type 2
	3	=	Type 3
	4	=	Type [Engineers reference]
M	1	=	corrugated beam
	2	=	open box beam
	3	=	open box beam with standard stiffeners
	4	=	open gox beam with non-standard stiffeners [Engineers reference]
	5	=	rectangular hollow section beam size 100mm × 100mm
	6	=	rectangular hollow section beam size 100m × 200mm
N	1	=	single sided
	2	=	double sided
	3	=	top fixed
	4	=	side fixed
O	1	=	Wooden
	2	=	Steel
	3	=	Steel fixed height
	4	=	Steel adjustable height [Engineers reference]
	5	=	Steel non-standard height [Engineers reference]
	6	=	Non-standard [Engineers reference]
P	0	=	No entry
	1	=	with off-set brackets [Engineers reference]
	2	=	with standard spacers
	3	=	with non-standard spacers [Engineers reference]
Q	0	=	No entry
	1	=	on adaptor platform [Engineers reference]
R	1 etc =		[Engineers reference]
S	1	=	rock
	2	=	reinforced concrete
T	1 etc =		[appropriate code derived from Drawings for Fence]
U	1 etc =		[each type of fence]

Notes

General
1 The following information should be shown on the Drawings for each type of stated temporary, permanent motorway, accommodation and safety fencing :

(a) The position and length of fencing identified by the use of the reference numbers or codes given or derived from Standard Drawings as appropriate;
(b) The height of permanent motorway and accommodation fencing;
(c) Concrete footings to intermediate posts where required by the Engineer;
(d) Painted lengths of fencing;
(e) In the case of safety fencing, the position of each type of fitting identified by the code given on Standard Drawings as appropriate.

The type and location of each type of gate and stile should also be shown on the Drawings together with the height and width of gates and any requirements for painting.

Temporary Fencing

2 The Measurement Clauses coupled with the Specification Clauses clarify the situation in respect of temporary fencing. They should reduce the pressure on the Engineer to authorise the use of an payment for temporary fencing and at the same time leave the usage to an economic choice by the Contractor. The Drawings should indicate all specific locations where stated temporary fencing of a semi-permanent nature is required during the construction period to meet particular needs, eg to isolate a semi-permanent diversion of a public right of way. Such stated temporary fencing being additional to the Contractors obligations under 19 and 22 of the ICE Conditions of Contract 5th Edition should be billed.

Fences Gates and Stiles

3 Code numbers for fencing derived from Standard Drawings should be given in addition to the relevant item description.
The different heights of fences and heights and widths of gates referred to above are shown on the Standard Drawings but in order to achieve a degree of standardisation measurement should be based on the following:

	Height	Width
Fences	As appropriate from those listed in the tables on Standard Drawings	
Steel Tubular Gates	From underside of bottom rail to top of top rail	From outer edge of hanging stile to outer edge of shutting stile except for double field gates when it should be to the outer edge of both hanging stiles

| Timber Gates including Kissing and Wicket Gates | Overall length of hanging stile | As for steel tubular gates above. |

Safety Fences

4 The MMRB requires posts and mounting brackets to be measured separately from the beams which they support.

Where more than one type of beam is used on any one contract the posts, mounting brackets and fittings should be billed following either the beams they support or in the case of fittings the beams to which they are attached.

The measurement of the fittings includes, where appropriate, the necessary posts.

Where the Engineer requires the use of a 100 mm × 100 mm rectangular hollow section safety fence in central reserves, then the work required to harden such reserves should be measured in the appropriate MMRB Section. Where however the Contractor offers such a beam as an alternative in central reserves then the Engineer should check with the Contractor to ensure that he has allowed for the cost of hardening the reserves in his alternative proposal.

In the Specification Notes for Guidance on Clauses 408–412 reference is made in paragraph 5 to a two rail open box beam safety fence with added height and strength. Because this two tier type of fence is not shown on any Standard Drawings the MMRB will require amending to accommodate the measurement of such fences.

Section 5: Drainage and Service Ducts

Item	Root Narratives	Unit
	Sewers, Drains, Piped Culverts and Ducts (excluding French Drains)	
1	Connection of *A* diameter pipe to existing *A* diameter sewer or drain.	No
2	Connection of *A* diameter pipe to existing manhole or catchpit.	No
3	Connection of permanently severed *A* diameter land drain to new *A* diameter sewer or drain.	No
4	*A* diameter sewer or drain specified permitted design Group *B C D E.*	lin m
5	*A* diameter *F* in sewer or drain *G C D E.*	lin m
6	Adjustment on last item for variation greater than 150 mm above or below the average depth of................. (*depth as calculated*) per 25 mm of variation in excess of 150 mm.	lin m (rate only required)
7	*A* diameter *F* in piped culvert *G C D E.*	lin m
8	*A* diameter service duct specified permitted design Group *O C D E.*	lin m
9	*A* diameter *F* in service duct *H C D E.*	lin m
	French Drains	
10	Connection of *A* diameter pipe to existing *A* diameter sewer or drain.	No
11	Connection of *A* diameter pipe to existing manhole or catchpit.	No
12	*A* diameter french drain specified permitted design Group *B C D E.*	lin m
13	*A* diameter french drain specified permitted design Type *I C D E.*	lin m
14	*A* diameter *F* french drain with *H* and *J* filter material *C D E.*	lin m
15	Adjustment on last item for variation greater than 150 mm above or below the average depth of.................(*depth as calculated*) per 25 mm of variation in excess of 150 mm.	(rate only required)
16	*J* filter material contiguous with french drain.	cu m
	Manholes, Catchpits, Drawpits and Gullies	
17	Manhole specified permitted design group *K* with *L* and frame depth to invert *M*	No

Item	Root Narratives	Unit
18	*N* Manhole *O* with *L* and frame depth to invert *M*.	No
19	Catchpit specified permitted design group *K* with *L* and frame depth to uppermost surface of base slab *M*.	No
20	*N* catchpit *O* with *L* and frame depth to uppermost surface of base slab *M*.	No
21	*N* drawpit *O* with *L* and frame depth to uppermost surface of base slab *M*.	No
22	*P* street gully specified permitted design group *O* with *L* and frame.	No
23	*Q P* street gully with *L* and frame.	No

Intercepting Ditches

24	Excavation of intercepting ditches.	cu m
25	Lining of *R* to intercepting ditches with *S T*.	sq m

Excavation in Rock and Reinforced Concrete

26	Extra over any item of drainage for excavation in *U*	cu m

Reinstatement of Pavement

27	Extra over *A* diameter sewer, drain or service duct for reinstating *V* pavement and foundation under.	lin m

Soft Spots and Other Voids

28	Excavation of soft spots in bottom of trenches, manholes, catchpits, draw pits and gullies.	cu m
29	Filling of soft spot and other voids in bottom of trenches, manholes, catchpits, draw pits and gullies with *W*.	cu m

Supports left in Excavation

30	Timber supports in construction *X*.	sq m
31	Steel sheeting supports left in construction *X*.	sq m

Drainage and Ducts in Bridges, Viaducts and Other Structures

32	*Y* substructure—End supports.	Item
33	*Y* substructure—Intermediate supports.	Item
34	*Y* superstructure.	Item
35	*Y* (in other structures).	Item

Filling to Pipe Bays on Bridges

36	Filling to pipe bays on bridges with *Z*.	cu m

Group	Variables			
A	1	=	100 mm	
	2	=	150 mm	
	3	=	225 mm	
	4	=	300 mm	
	5	=	375 mm	
	6	=	450 mm	
	7	=	525 mm	
	8	=	600 mm	
	9	=	675 mm	
	10	=	750 mm	
	11	=	825 mm	
	12	=	900 mm	
	13	=	One number 100 mm	
	14	=	Two number 100 mm	(For Ducts only)
	15	=	Three number 100 mm	
	16	=	Four number 100 mm	

Group	Variables			
B	1	=	1	Note: These group reference numbers
	2	=	2	allow for all types of bed combination.
		=	3	Where a particular bed is excluded from
	4	=	4	any one Group, the Group reference
	5	=	5	should be followed by the suffix X and
	6	=	6	the excluded bed type eg 3XD.
	7	=	7	
	8	=	8	
	9	=	9	
	10	=	10	
	11	=	11	
	12	=	12	
	13	=	13	
	14	=	14	
	15	=	15	
	16	=	16	
	17	=	17	
	18	=	18	

Group	Variables		
C	1	=	in trench
	2	=	in heading
	3	=	by jacking or thrust boring
	4	=	suspended on discrete supports [Drawing No.]

Group	Variables		
D	0	=	No entry
	1	=	in sides slopes of cutting or embankments

Group	Variables		
E	1	=	depth to invert of 1·5 metres of less
	2	=	depth to invert of 1·5 metres or less average depth to invert .... [depth as calculated to the nearest 25 mm]

Group		Variables	
E contd.	**3**	=	depth to invert of over 1·5 metres average depth to invert .... [depth as calculated to the the nearest 25 mm] maximum depth to invert .... [depth as calculated to the nearest 25 mm]
F	*1*	=	clay pipes standard strength
	2	=	clay pipes extra strength
	3	=	clay pipes super strength
	4	=	perforated clay pipes
	5	=	concrete standard pipes
	6	=	concrete pipes extra strength Class L
	7	=	concrete pipes extra strength Class M
	8	=	concrete pipes extra strength Class H
	9	=	perforated concrete pipes
	10	=	porous concrete pipes
	11	=	asbestos cement pipes Class L
	12	=	asbestos cement pipes Class M
	13	=	asbestos cement pipes Class H
	14	=	perforated or slotted asbestos pipes
	15	=	pitch fibre pipes
	16	=	perforated pitch fibre pipes
	17	=	UPVC Class B pipes
	18	=	UPVC Class C pipes
	19	=	UPVC Class D pipes
	20	=	perforated or slotted UPVC pipes
	21	=	ductile cast iron Class K9 pipes
	22	=	corrugated metal pipes
	23	=	perforated corrugated metal pipe
	24	=	vitrified clay ⎫
	25	=	UPVC ⎪ (For Ducts only)
	26	=	galvanised steel Class H ⎬
	27	=	ductile cast iron ⎭
G	*1*	=	on bed Type A
	2	=	on bed Type B
	3	=	on bed Type D
	4	=	on bed Type E
	5	=	on bed Type N
	6	=	on bed Type Q
	7	=	on bed Type Z
	8 etc	=	[Engineers reference for bed type]
H	*1* etc	=	[Engineers reference for bed and surround]
I	*1*	=	Type F
	2	=	Type G
	3	=	Type H

Group	Variables		
I contd.	**4**	=	Type J
	5	=	Type K
	6	=	Type L
	7	=	Type M
	8 etc =		[Engineers Type reference]
J	**1**	=	Type A
	2	=	Type B
K	**1**	=	Type 1
	2	=	Type 2
	3	=	Type 3
	4	=	Type 4
	5	=	Type 5
	6	=	Type 6
	7	=	Type 7
	8	=	Type 8
	9 etc =		Type [Engineers group reference]
L	**1**	=	Grade A cover
	2	=	Grade B cover
	3	=	Grade D grating
	4	=	[Engineers type reference]
M	**1**	=	2 metres or less
	2 etc =		exceeding 2 metres but not exceeding 3 metres (and so on in stages of 1 metre)
N	**1**	=	Brick
	2	=	Precast concrete
	3	=	In situ concrete 22·5/37·5
O	**1**	=	[Engineers group reference for ducts]
	2	=	[Engineers type reference for manholes, catchpits, drawpits and street gullies]
P	**1**	=	Trapped
	2	=	Untrapped
Q	**1**	=	Precast concrete
	2	=	Salt glazed stoneware
	3	=	Vitrified clay
	4	=	Cast iron
	5	=	In situ concrete 22·5/20 with plastic former
R	**1**	=	inverts
	2	=	side slopes

Group	Variables		
S	**1**	=	precast concrete
	2	=	granite setts
	3	=	concrete class 30/20
	4	=	uncoursed random rubble
T	**0**	=	No entry
	1	=	25 mm thick
	2	=	50 mm thick
	3 etc =		75 mm thick and so in steps of 25 mm
U	**1**	=	rock
	2	=	reinfoced concrete
V	**1** etc =		[Engineers reference for different types of rein-statement]
W	**1**	=	pipe bedding material
	2	=	type 1 sub-base material
	3	=	Class E concrete fill
X	**0**	=	No entry
	1	=	in trench
	2	=	in pits
	3	=	in heading
Y	**1**	=	Drainage of
	2	=	Ducts in
Z	**1**	=	granular material
	2 etc =		[Engineers stated material]

Notes

General

1 Attention is drawn to the Notes for Guidance on Section 6: Earthworks in which the Earthworks Outline is shown in diagrammatic form.

The composite method of billing requires all the relevant information to be shown on the drawings.

To assist Tenderers the Drainage Schedule should also show the computation of the average depth.

Any excavated suitable material which is surplus to the backfilling requirement of this Section, should not be taken into account when balancing the earthworks in Section 6: Earthworks. It is assumed that Tenderers will make due allowance for this in their rates and prices.

It should be noted that a distinction has been made in the MMRB between the computation of depths for drain trenches and the excavation in rock and reinforced concrete in those trenches.

Sewers, Drains, Piped
Culverts and Ducts
(Excluding
French Drains)

2 For drains of depth to invert of 1·5 metres or less support of the trench sides is rarely necessary and in consequence the cost of constructing these drains largely unrelated to minor depth changes. For deeper drains with depth to invert of over 1·5 metres the cost will vary with depth changes and it is for this reason that the rate for each 25 mm of difference (in excess of 150 mm) is required.

Where the depth to invert necessitates a change in the class of pipe or construction this should be shown on the Drawings. Where the number of pipe fittings is likely to be high relative to the drain length, as in urban areas, pipe fittings should, at the Engineer's discretion, be measured by number as extra over the drain or sewer. The MMRB will require amending by a Preamble in the Bill of Quantities if this way of measuring is adopted.

The MMRB does not cater for the measurement of two separate sewers or drain pipes laid in one trench. If this is required the MMRB should be amended.

Piping of culverts, the designs of which are simple and more akin to sewers and drains, should be measured in this Section whilst those of a complex design should be measured as 'Other Structures'.

Where more than one duct is laid in a trench, the Drawings should clearly show the configuration of ducts within that trench. Only one linear measurement should however be taken for the complete trench with the number of ducts stated in the item description.

French Drains

3 Because of the cost of filter material the rate for each 25 mm of difference (in excess of 150 mm) is required after each item for french drain runs irrespective of the depth to invert.

Manholes, Catchpits,
Draw pits and Gullies

4 Standard manhole designs (at least for a particular contract) should be prepared which will require only variations of depth for each design type. Manholes with backdrops should be separately identified.

A schedule of manholes, catchpits, drawpits and gullies should be prepared showing the groups of permitted alternatives and/or particular designs, individual depths and their locations. They should be collected into the depths stated in the MMRB.

Headwalls and
Outfall Works

5 Quantities for similar items or work for headwalls and outfalls to pipes of 2 metres internal diameter or less should be aggregated and billed in this Section with the number of headwall and outfall works stated. Headwall and outfall works to pipes of over 2 metres internal diameter should each be classified as 'Other Structures' and billed accordingly.

Drainage and Ducts in Bridges, Viaducts and Other Structures

6 Substructure and superstructure drainage and ducts should be clearly identified and quantified on the Drawings preferably on separate drainage schedules.

The lump sum items for such drainage and ducts should be included in the bridge works sections of the Bill of Quantities under the appropriate sub-heading.

The facility of using single lump-sum items for drainage and ducts to bridges, viaducts and other structures is intended to be applied in cases where the work involved is simple in character and where the extent of the work to be included in an item can be clearly shown on the Drawings. Otherwise the system should be measured in detail following the philosophy of the MMRB. The Bill of Quantities should incorporate the necessary preamble amending the MMRB in this respect. Both methods of measurement may be used in any one Contract but only one method should be used for any one bridge or structure.

Testing

7 Drains and surface water drains with water tight joints are according to clause 509(i) of the Specification only required to be tested as directed by the Engineer. It is for this reason that the item coverage no longer includes testing and also why the Notes for Guidance on that clause refer to inserting of provisional items in the Bill of Quantities.

Section 6: Earthworks

Item	Root Narratives	Unit
	Excavation	
1	Excavate topsoil.	cu m
2	Excavate **A** in cuttings and excavation in bulk in the open.	cu m
3	Excavate **A** in structural foundations **B** in depth.	cu m
4	Excavate **A** in new watercourses.	cu m
5	Excavate **A** in enlarged watercourses.	cu m
6	Excavate **A** in clearing abandoned watercourses.	cu m
	Deposition of Fill	
7	Deposition of **CE**.	cu m
	Disposal of Material	
8	Disposal of **D** in tips off Site.	cu m
	Imported Fill	
9	**F** deposited **E**.	cu m
	Compaction of Fill	
10	Compaction of **GE**.	cu m
	Soft Spots and Other Voids	
11	Excavation of soft spots **I**.	cu m
12	Filling of soft spots and other voids **I** with **J**.	cu m
	Supports Left in Excavation	
13	**H** supports left in excavation.	sq m
	Soiling	
14	Soiling **L** thick **K**.	sq m
	Grassing	
15	Grass Seeding **K**.	sq m
16	Turfing **K**.	sq m
17	'Hydraulic Mulch' grass seeding **K**.	sq m
	Completion of Formation	
18	Formation of suitable material.	sq m
19	Formation of rock fill.	sq m
20	Formation of rock cuttings **M**.	sq m

Item	Root Narratives	Unit
	Lining of Watercourses	
21	Lining to **N** of **O** watercourse with **PL** thick.	sq m
	Clearance of Existing Ditches	
22	Clear existing ditch at **Q.**	lin m

Group	Variables		
A	*1*	=	suitable material except rock
	2	=	unsuitable material
	3	=	rock
	4	=	reinforced concrete
B	*1*	=	0 metres to 3 metres
	2	=	0 metres to 6 metres
	3 etc =		0 metres to 9 metres and so on in steps of 3 metres
C	*1*	=	suitable material
	2	=	rock fill
D	*1*	=	suitable material
	2	=	unsuitable material
E	*1*	=	in embankments and other areas of fill other than adjacent to structures
	2	=	on sub-base material under verges, central reserves and side slopes.
	3	=	into soft areas
	4	=	around structural foundations
	5	=	adjacent to structures excluding around foundations
	6	=	on bridges (under footways, verges and central reserves)
F	*1*	=	imported suitable material fill
	2	=	imported granular fill
	3	=	imported free draining material
	4	=	imported rock fill
	5 etc =		[Engineers requirement for other types of imported fill]
G	*1*	=	fill material
	2	=	rock fill
H	*1*	=	timber
	2	=	steel sheeting
I	*1*	=	below cuttings or under embankments
	2	=	in rock in side slopes
	3	=	below structural foundations

Group	Variables		
J	**1**	=	suitable material fill
	2	=	granular fill
	3	=	rock fill
	4	=	concrete fill
	5	=	masonry fill
K	**1**	=	to surfaces sloping at 10° or less to the horizontal
	2	=	to surfaces sloping at more than 10° to the horizontal
L	**1**	=	25 mm
	2	=	50 mm
	3	=	75 mm
	4 etc =		100 mm
			(and so on steps of 25 mm)
M	**1**	=	regulated with lean concrete
	2	=	regulated with sub base material
N	**1**	=	inverts
	2	=	side slops
O	**1**	=	new
	2	=	enlarged
P	**1**	=	precast concrete
	2	=	granite setts
	3	=	concrete class 30/20
	4	=	uncoursed random rubble
	5	=	coursed random rubble
Q	**1** etc =		[Engineers locational reference]

Notes

General

1 The Earthworks Outline, defined in paragraph 5 and 6 of this Section of the MMRB is shown for typical cross sections of a road, at Figure 1 on page 36 hereof.

Earthworks Quantities

2 The Notes for Guidance on the Specification Series 600 Earthworks at sub-paragraphs 9 (iii) and (iv) propose that the fullest available construction information should be given to Tenderers. It is suggested that the Drawings would be the most convenient place to give the Tenderers the quantities and anticipated types of material to be encountered in each location.

In order to arrive at the billed quantities it is necessary to collect the earthworks information into Schedules, examples of which are given in Figure 2 for Structures and Figure 3 for Roadworks. Separate schedules should be prepared for both Flexible and Rigid construction where alternative tenders are required. Because of the wide divergence of requirements and circumstances between contracts the schedules cannot cater for every situation. They can only illustrate the type of headings and information required and should therefore be amended and adapted to suit the particular requirement and circumstances applying to any one contract. Similarly the Tables 1 to 5 inclusive can only give guidance on how to arrive at the billed quantities.

The various materials arising from the excavations for new, enlarged and clearing abandoned water courses should be shown separately from but immediately following the location in which they lie or are adjacent to.

The initial information which should be entered in the schedules are the quantities of excavation of all types, compacted fill, specified rock fill and imported fill in all locations. From these overall totals for the contract the surplus or shortfall in the quantity of suitable material arising from or required for the works can be established. This is shown in Tables 1 to 3 inclusive. With this point established the quantities of suitable material for deposition can be found for each location by following the procedures shown in Tables 4 and 5. Total deposition in all locations will however only be equal to the volume of suitable material available as fill from the Site. For this reason Table 4 illustrates the calculation of deposition, in this case in embankments when imported fill is involved. The volume of suitable material for disposal or the requirements of imported fill should be ascertained by following the procedures shown in Table 3.

Engineers should ensure that the earthworks requirements over the contract as a whole balance eg: the total quantity of material excavated (other than top soil) should equal the summated quantities for deposition and disposal.

Deposition of Fill

3 The volumes of all earthworks materials (other than top soil) which are placed directly on sub-base material should be measured as material deposited and compacted 'on sub-base material under verges, central reserves and side slopes' to the extent shown on the drawings.

Compaction of Fill

4 The compaction of fill material deposited below water should be measured in order that quantities of such filling can be taken into account in the earthworks balance.

Grass Seeding and Turfing

5 In order to avoid the necessity for linear measurements turf widths are not stated.

Fig.1.

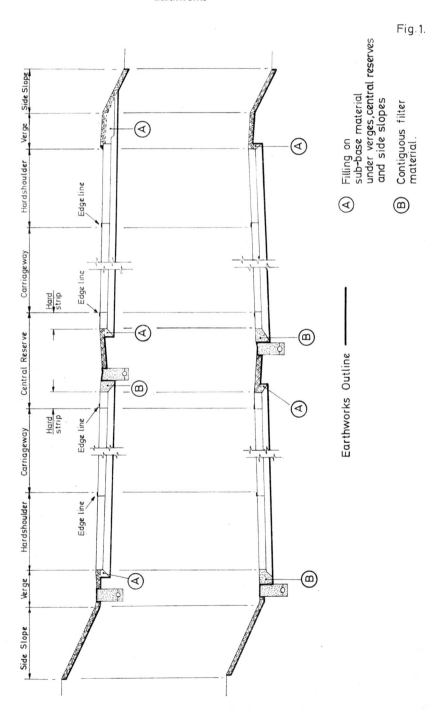

Earthworks Outline ——————

(A) Filling on
      sub-base material
      under verges, central reserves
      and side slopes

(B) Contiguous filter
      material.

FIGURE 2

STRUCTURES EARTHWORKS SCHEDULE

LOCATION	EXCAVATION					FILL											
	Volume of material suitable except rock in structural foundations	Volume of material unsuitable in structural foundations	Volume of rock in structural foundations	Volume of reinforced concrete in structural foundations	Total volume of excavation excluding top soil in structural foundations	Volume of Suitable Material Fill			Volume of Specified Rock Fill		Volume of Free Draining Fill Material		Volume of Granular Fill Material		Total Volume of Compaction of Fill		
						Adjacent to structures excluding around foundations	Around structural foundations	On bridges under footways verges and central reserves	Adjacent to structures excluding around foundations	Around structural foundations	Adjacent to structures excluding around foundations	Around structural foundations	Adjacent to structures excluding around foundations	Around structural foundations	Adjacent to structures excluding around foundations	Around structural foundations	On bridges under footways verges and central reserves
	1	2	3	4	5	6	7	8	9	10	11	12	13	14	15	16	17
Sub Totals																	
Structures Totals																	

FIGURE 3

ROADWORKS EARTHWORKS SCHEDULE

LOCATION	EXCAVATION								FILL									
					Volume of Unsuitable Material				Volume of Specified Rock Fill		Volume of Free Draining Fill Material			Volume of Granular Fill Material				
	Volume of top soil	Volume of suitable material except rock	Volume of rock	Volume of reinforced concrete	Above Earthworks Outline	Below Earthworks Outline	Under Embankments	Total volume of excavation excluding top soil	In embankments	Into soft areas	In embankments	Into soft areas	On sub-base under verges etc	In embankments	Into soft areas	On sub-base under verges etc	Total volume of compaction of fill in embankments	Total volume of compaction of fill on sub-base under verges etc
	1	2	3	4	5	6	7	8	9	10	11	12	13	14	15	16	17	18
Chainage A to B Watercourses New Enlarged Abandoned																		
Sub Totals																		
Roadworks Totals																		

TABLE 1: To ascertain rock situation over contract as a whole.

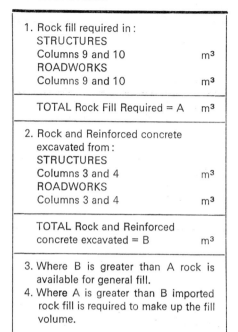

1. Rock fill required in: STRUCTURES Columns 9 and 10 ROADWORKS Columns 9 and 10	m³ m³
TOTAL Rock Fill Required = A	m³
2. Rock and Reinforced concrete excavated from: STRUCTURES Columns 3 and 4 ROADWORKS Columns 3 and 4	m³ m³
TOTAL Rock and Reinforced concrete excavated = B	m³

3. Where B is greater than A rock is available for general fill.
4. Where A is greater than B imported rock fill is required to make up the fill volume.

TABLE 2: To ascertain requirements of suitable fill material taking all structures as an entity.

1. Suitable material fill required: Columns 6 to 8 = C	m³
2. Excavated suitable material: Column 1 = D	m³

3. The surplus (D greater than C) or shortfall (C greater than D) should be carried to Table 3 opposite.

NOTE: In the case of a shortfall the deposition of suitable material, from elsewhere on site and compaction shall be measured with Structures.

TABLE 3: To ascertain suitable material situation over contract as a whole.

1. Excavated suitable material from ROADWORKS Column 2 Rock available for use as General fill from Table 1 opposite Add Surplus or Deduct shortfall from Structures Table 2 opposite	m³ m³ m³
TOTAL Suitable Material available = E	m³
2. TOTAL Volume of Compacted fill in ROADWORKS Columns 17 and 18 Deduct Volumes of fill other than Suitable in ROADWORKS Columns 9, 11, 13, 14 and 16	m³ m³
TOTAL Suitable Material required = F	m³

3. Where F is greater than E imported suitable material is required. (See Table 4 page 40.)
4. Where E is greater than F there is suitable material for disposal.

NOTE: In the case of surplus suitable from Structures deposition, compaction or disposal as appropriate shall be measured with the Roadworks.

TABLE 4: Example of the Calculation of quantities for deposition of suitable material in embankments.

TOTAL Volume of compaction fill material in embankments Column 17 = G $\quad$ m³
Volume of fill material other than suitable material in embankments Columns 9, 11 and 14 = H $\quad$ m³
Volume of suitable fill material required in embankments G–H $\quad$ m³
Volume of imported fill See Table 3 page 39 = J $\quad$ m³
Volume of deposition = G— (H +J) $\quad$ m³

TABLE 5: Examples of the Calculation of quantities for deposition of suitable material around structural foundations.

TOTAL Volume of compaction of fill material around structural foundations Column 16 = K $\quad$ m³
Volume of fill material other than suitable material around structural foundations Columns 10, 12 and 14 = L $\quad$ m³
Volume of deposition of suitable material around structural foundations KL— $\quad$ m³

Explanatory Note
1 A careful estimate should be made of the volume of rock fill deposited in soft areas for Roadworks Schedule Columns 10, 12 and 15 (see Specification clause 604 (2).

Section 7: Roadworks Overall Requirements

General

Notes

1 No bill items should be provided for complying with the requirements of the Series No. 700 Clauses of the Specification.

Section 8: Sub-base and Roadbase

Item	Root Narratives	Unit
1	*A* sub-base *G*	cu m
2	*B* roadbase *E* thick *FG.*	sq m
3	*C* regulating course (conversion factor........ cubic metre per tonne) *G.*	tonne
4	*D* regulating course *G.*	cu m

Group	Variables		
A	1	=	Group A
	2	=	Group B
	3	=	Group C
	4	=	Granular Type 1
	5	=	Granular Type 2
	6	=	Soil cement
	7	=	Cement bound granular
	8	=	Lean concrete
	9	=	Wet lean concrete
B	1	=	Group D
	2	=	Group E
	3	=	Group F
	4	=	Group G
	5	=	Group H
	6	=	Soil cement
	7	=	Cement bound granular
	8	=	Lean concrete
	9	=	Wet mix macadam
	10	=	Dry bound macadam 40 mm coarse aggregate
	11	=	Dry bound macadam 50 mm coarse aggregate
	12	=	Dense tarmacadam
	13	=	Dense bitumen macadam
	14	=	Rolled asphalt
C	1	=	Wet mix macadam
	2	=	Dry bound macadam
	3	=	Dense tarmacadam
	4	=	Dense bitumen macadam
	5	=	Rolled asphalt
	6	=	Bitumen macadam

Group	Variables		
C contd.	*7*	=	Tarmacadam
	8	=	[Engineers group reference]
D	*1*	=	Soil cement
	2	=	Cement bound granular
	3	=	Lean concrete
	4	=	[Engineers group reference]
E	*1*	=	60 mm
	2	=	70 mm
	3	=	80 mm
	4	=	90 mm
	5	=	100 mm
	6	=	110 mm
	7	=	115 mm
	8	=	120 mm
	9	=	130 mm
	10	=	135 mm
	11	=	140 mm
	12	=	150 mm
	13	=	155 mm
	14	=	160 mm
	15	=	170 mm
	16	=	180 mm
	17	=	185 mm
	18	=	190 mm
	19	=	205 mm
	20	=	210 mm
	21	=	220 mm
	22	=	230 mm
	23	=	245 mm
	24	=	250 mm
	25	=	260 mm
F	*1*	=	in carriageway
	2	=	in hard shoulder
G	*0*	=	No entry
	1 etc =		[Engineers carriageway identification reference]

Notes

General

1 The method of measurement is based on the measurement of structural elements of a pavement rather than individual layers.

Specification Clause 801 gives all the generally permitted alternative materials by Groups for sub-bases and roadbases and will effectively give the contractor the choice of using any of these alternative materials.

The measurement should, however, always be based on the thinnest permitted alternatives in accordance with Preamble 4 to the Bill of Quantities.

Variable G has been included in the library to facilitate the separate identification of lengths of carriageway with:

(a) the same alternative permitted material Group references but with different msa's and correspondingly different range of construction thickness; and/or

(b) different polished stone values; and/or

(c) any additional limitations stated in the Contract.

Such lengths of carriageway should be separately identified in the location column in the Pavement Thickness Schedule (see Specification Notes for Guidance, Table 4) and it is recommended that a number be allocated to each of these locational references. This number can then be quoted in the item description in lieu of the fully descriptive locational reference.

Sub-base

2 Bill items for sub-base should describe the Group of permitted alternative materials from Table 8/1 of Specification Clause 801 and the thickness to be provided should be shown on the Drawings.

Roadbase

3 Bill items for roadbase should describe the Group of permitted alternative materials from Table 8/2 of the Specification Clause 801 and the thickness required.

Attention is drawn to the fact that when the Groups from Table 8/2 are cross referenced to the Design Table in the Notes for Guidance to the Specification, it will be seen that Group D in Table 1 covers the full range of msa's from 2·5 to 80, whilst Groups E, F and G in Table 2 only cover certain bands of msa's. When the Engineer permits the full range of roadbase alternatives the single Group reference quoted in the bill item and in the Pavement Thickness Schedule should always be the letter indicated in Table 2. (For example, at 9 MSA Table 1 indicates Group D and Table 2, Group F. Since Group F is defined as including Group D the Group reference would be F while the thickness specified would be that taken from Table 1.)

Regulating Course

4 When the Engineer wishes to provide the Contractor with a choice of regulating materials the Drawings should indicate the permitted alternatives and be cross referenced to the bill item by a Group or Type letter or number.

Section 9: Flexible Surfacing

Item	Root Narratives	Unit
1	Flexible surfacing permitted alternative materials **AB** total thickness **GH.**	sq m
2	Flexible surfacing comprising of **C** base course **B** thick and **D** wearing course **B** thick **GH.**	sq m
3	Flexible surfacing comprising of **C** base course **B** thick and **D** wearing course **B** thick with **E** coated chippings **GH.**	sq m
4	Flexible surfacing comprising of **C** base course **B** thick and slurry sealing **E** thick **GH.**	sq m
5	Flexible surfacing comprising of **C** base course **B** thick and surface dressing **FGH.**	sq m
6	**C** base course **B** thick **GH.**	sq m
7	**C** base regulating course **G** (conversion factor.........cubic metre per tonne) **H.**	tonne
8	**D** wearing course **B** thick **GH.**	sq m
9	**D** wearing course **B** thick with **E** coated chippings **GH.**	sq m
10	Slurry sealing **E** thick **G.**	sq m
11	Surface dressing **FG.**	sq m
12	Bituminous spray **FG.**	sq m

Group	Variables		
A	1	=	Group V
	2	=	Group W
	3	=	Group Y
	4	=	Group Z
B	1	=	20 mm
	2	=	25 mm
	3	=	30 mm
	4	=	35 mm
	5	=	40 mm
	6	=	50 mm
	7	=	60 mm
	8	=	70 mm
	9	=	75 mm
	10	=	80 mm
	11	=	85 mm
	12	=	90 mm
	13	=	95 mm

Group	Variables		
B contd.	*14*	=	100 mm
	15	=	105 mm
	16	=	110 mm
	17	=	115 mm
	18	=	125 mm
	19	=	130 mm
	20	=	140 mm
	21	=	145 mm
C	*1*	=	Rolled asphalt
	2	=	Dense bitumen macadam 20 mm aggregate
	3	=	Dense bitumen macadam 28 mm aggregate
	4	=	Dense bitumen macadam 40 mm aggregate
	5	=	Dense tarmacadam 20 mm aggregate
	6	=	Dense tarmacadam 28 mm aggregate
	7	=	Dense tarmacadam 40 mm aggregate
	8	=	Bitumen macadam
	9	=	Tarmacadam
	10	=	[Engineers group reference]
D	*1*	=	Rolled asphalt
	2	=	Dense bitumen macadam 10 mm aggregate
	3	=	Dense bitumen macadam 14 mm aggregate
	4	=	Dense tar surfacing 10 mm aggregate
	5	=	Dense tar surfacing 14 mm aggregate
	6	=	Cold asphalt
	7	=	Open textured bitumen macadam 10 mm aggregate
	8	=	Open textured bitumen macadam 14 mm aggregate
	9	=	Open textured tarmacadam 10 mm aggregate
	10	=	Open textured tarmacadam 14 mm aggregate
	11	=	[Engineers group reference]
E	*1*	=	1·5 mm
	2	=	3 mm
	3	=	14 mm
	4	=	20 mm
F	*1* etc =		[Engineers specification reference]
G	*1*	=	in carriageway
	2	=	in hard shoulder
H	*1*	=	No entry
	2 etc =		[Engineers carriageway identification reference]

Notes

General

1 The appropriate flexible surfacing group depending on traffic should be specified in the Contract for each category of road. These groups are given in Table 9/1 of the Specification and Design Tables 1 and 2 of the Notes for Guidance on the Specification.

Variable H has been included in the library to facilitate the separate identification of lengths of carriageway with:

(a) the same alternative permitted material Group references but with different msa's and correspondingly different ranges of construction thickness; and/or

(b) different polished stone values and texture depths; and/or

(c) any additional limitations stated in the Contract.

Such lengths of carriageway should be separately identified in the location column in the Pavement Thickness Schedule (see Specification Notes for Guidance, Table 4) and it is recommended that a number be allocated to each of these locational references. This number can then be quoted in the item description in lieu of the fully descriptive locational reference.

Flexible Surfacing

2 Bill items should be for the complete surfacing with the total thickness of the combined basecourse and wearing course being stated including the thickness of any surface dressing which is specified as part of the group.

Provision is also made in the library for the measurement of the two courses separately eg tie-ins between new and old work.

Regulating Course

3 When the Engineer wishes to provide the Contractor with a choice of regulating materials the Drawings should indicate the permitted alternatives and be cross referenced to the bill item by a Group or Type letter or number.

Slurry Sealing
Surface Dressing
and Bituminous Spray

4 Each type of surface dressing and bituminous spray to to specification Clause 915 and 916 respectively should be cross reference to the bill item by a Group or Type letter or number.

Section 10: Concrete Pavement

Item	Root Narratives	Unit
1	*A* concrete carriageway *B* thick *C*	sq m
2	*A* concrete hard shoulder *B* thick *C*.	sq m

Group	Variables		
A	*1*	=	Specified permitted alternative design for
	2	=	Reinforced
	3	=	Unreinforced
B	*1*	=	130 mm
	2	=	140 mm
	3	=	150 mm
	4	=	160 mm
	5	=	165 mm
	6	=	170 mm
	7	=	180 mm
	8	=	185 mm
	9	=	190 mm
	10	=	200 mm
	11	=	210 mm
	12	=	215 mm
	13	=	220 mm
	14	=	225 mm
	15	=	230 mm
	16	=	235 mm
	17	=	240 mm
	18	=	245 mm
	19	=	250 mm
	20	=	255 mm
	21	=	260 mm
	22	=	265 mm
	23	=	270 mm
	24	=	280 mm
	25	=	290 mm
	26	=	300 mm
	27	=	305 mm
C	*1* etc =		[Engineers Drawing number reference]

General

Notes

1 Alternative designs and Bills of Quantities should be prepared for flexible and rigid pavement construction in accordance with paragraph 7 of Structural Design of Pavements in the Notes for Guidance on the Specification and the Standard Drawings.

Where the design thickness for reinforced and unreinforced rigid pavement constructions differs, only the thinnest of the permitted alternatives should be billed.

Section 11: Kerbs and Footways

Item	Root Narratives	Unit
	Kerbing Channelling and Edging	
1	Specified permitted alternative kerbing Group *AB*	lin m
2	*C* kerbing *DB*	lin m
3	*C* channelling *DB*	lin m
4	Specified permitted alternative edging Group *AB*	lin m
5	*C* edging *DB*	lin m
	Excavation in Rock and Reinforced Concrete	
6	Extra over any item of kerbing, channelling or edging for excavation in *E*	cu m
	Footways	
7	*F* precast concrete paved footway on *G* sub-base *H* thick	sq m

Group	Variables		
A	*1* etc =		[Engineers Group number or letter reference]
B	*1*	=	laid straight or curved over 12 metres radius
	2	=	laid to curves of 12 metres radius or less
C	*1*	=	Precast concrete
	2	=	In-situ concrete
	3	=	Extruded concrete
	4	=	In-situ asphalt
	5	=	Extruded asphalt
D	*1* etc =		[Engineers type design reference]
E	*1*	=	rock
	2	=	reinforced concrete
	1	=	600 mm × 450 mm × 50 mm thick
	2	=	600 mm × 600 mm × 50 mm thick
	3	=	600 mm × 750 mm × 50 mm thick
	4	=	600 mm × 900 mm × 50 mm thick

G	*1* =	permitted alternative
	2 =	granular sub-base material type 1
	3 =	granular sub-base material type 2
	4 =	fine aggregate to BS882 Table 2 Zone 1
	5 =	fine aggregate to BS882 Table 2 Zone 2
	6 =	fine aggregate to BS882 Table 2 Zone 3
	7 =	fine aggregate to BS1201 Table 2 Zone 1
	8 =	fine aggregate to BS1201 Table 2 Zone 2
	9 =	clinker ash
H	*1* etc =	(required thickness)

Notes

Kerbing, Channelling and Edging

1 The Contractor should whenever possible be permitted the choice of type or method of kerbing and edging to be employed. The drawings should indicate the permitted alternatives and be cross referenced to the bill item by a Group letter or number.

Footways

2 Bill items for footways should include for the whole depth of construction.

Rock and Reinforced Concrete

3 Excavation for footways is measured in Section 6: Earthworks and the extra over items for excavation in rock and reinforced concrete therefore apply only to items for kerbs, channelling and edging.

Section 12: Traffic Signs and Road Markings

Item	Root Narratives	Unit
	Traffic Signs	
1	Standard **AB** traffic sign **C** approximately **D** in area and mounted on **EF**.	No
2	Non-standard **AB** traffic sign **C** approximately **D** in area and mounted on **EF**.	No
	Road Markings	
3	Solid area in **APGH**.	sq m
4	Continuous line in **APGHI** wide.	lin m
5	Intermittent line in **APGHI** wide with **I** line and **I** gap.	lin m
6	Ancillary line **APGHI** wide **J**.	lin m
7	Triangle in **APGH** diagram number 1023 of The Traffic Signs Regulation and General Directions.	No
8	Circle with enclosing arrows in **APGHI** diameter diagram number 1003. 4 of the Traffic Signs Regulations and General Directions.	No
9	Arrow in **APGHI** long **K** to **L**.	No
10	Kerb marking in **APGHI** long to **L**.	No
11	Letters in **APGHI** high.	No
12	Numerals in **APGHI** high.	No
	Road Studs	
13	**M N O** reflectorised road stud with **PQ** reflectors.	No
14	**MN** road stud.	No
	Marker Posts	
15	**R** marker post **S**.	No
	Excavation in Rock and Reinforced Concrete	
16	Extra over any item of traffic signs for excavation in **T**.	cu m

Group	Variables		
A	0	=	No entry
	1	=	reflectorised
	2	=	unreflectorised

Group	Variables		
B	0	=	No entry
	1	=	externally illuminated
	2	=	internally illuminated
C	1 etc =		[Engineers reference can be the identification generated in the schedule or from the Drawings or the Traffic Signs Regulations and General Directions diagram number]
D	1	=	0·25 square metre
	2	=	0·5 square metre
	3	=	0·75 square metre
	4	=	1 square metre
	5	=	2 square metres
	6	=	3 square metres
	7	=	4 square metres and so on in steps of 1 square metre
E	0	=	No entry
	1	=	existing
	2	=	separately measured
	3	=	one
	4	=	two
	5	=	three
	6	=	four
F	1	=	timber supporting post(s)
	2	=	reinforced concrete post(s)
	3	=	prestressed concrete post(s)
	4	=	rectangular steel posts(s)
	5	=	tubular steel post(s)
	6	=	bridge superstructure
	7	=	building
	8	=	gantry
G	1	=	chlorinated rubber paint
	2	=	one pack epoxy paint
	3	=	alkyd based paint
	4	=	thermo plastic screed
	5	=	thermo plastic spray
H	0	=	No entry
	1	=	with applied ballotini
I	1	=	50 mm
	2	=	60 mm
	3	=	75 mm
	4	=	100 mm

I contd	5	=	150 mm
	6	=	200 mm
	7	=	250 mm
	8	=	280 mm
	9	=	300 mm
	10	=	350 mm
	11	=	500 mm
	12	=	600 mm
	13	=	700 mm
	14	=	1000 mm
	15	=	1600 mm
	16	=	2000 mm
	17	=	2800 mm
	18	=	3000 mm
	19	=	3500 mm
	20	=	4000 mm
	21	=	4200 mm
	22	=	4500 mm
	23	=	5000 mm
	24	=	6000 mm
	25	=	7000 mm
	26	=	8000 mm
	27	=	9000 mm
	28	=	16 000 m
	29	=	32 000 mm
	30	=	[Engineers unique dimension]
J	1	=	in zigzags
	2	=	in hatched areas
	3	=	in chevrons
	4	=	in box areas
K	1	=	straight
	2	=	curved
	3	=	turning
	4	=	double headed
L	1	=	diagram number 1014 of the Traffic Signs Regulations and General Directions
	2	=	diagram number 1038 of the Traffic Signs Regulations and General Directions
	3	=	diagram number 1039 of the Traffic Signs Regulations and General Directions
	4	=	diagram number 1050 of the Traffic Signs Regulations and General Directions
	5	=	diagram number 1019 of the Traffic Signs Regulations and General Directions
	6	=	diagram number 1020 of the Traffic Signs Regulations and General Directions
	7	=	diagram number 1021 of the Traffic Signs Regulations and General Directions

Group	Variables		
M	**1** etc =		[size as required]
N	**1**	=	square
	2	=	circular
	3	=	rectangular
O	**1**	=	one way
	2	=	bi-directional
P	**1**	=	yellow
	2	=	white
	3	=	red
	4	=	green
	5	=	amber
Q	**0**	=	No entry
	1	=	corner cube
	2	=	convex lens
R	**1**	=	timber
	2	=	glass reinforced plastic
S	**1**	=	Type 1
	2	=	Type 2
	3	=	Type 3
	4	=	Type 4
	5	=	Type 5
	6	=	Type 6
	7	=	Type 7
	8	=	Type 8
	9	=	Type 9
T	**1**	=	rock
	2	=	reinforced concrete

Notes

Traffic Signs

1 Standard traffic signs should include those signs which have standard symbols and markings (with permitted variants). These signs are shown in The Traffic Signs Regulations and General Directions and will generally be selected from the 500, 600 and 800 series.

Non-standard traffic signs should include directional or other informatory signs which require specific symbols and markings for a particular location, and will generally be selected from the 700 and 900 series.

A schedule should be provided in the Contract quoting in the case of standard signs, the diagram number and where necessary the required permitted variant, the overall size of the sign or where no size is given, the height of the lettering required. In the case of non-standard signs the diagram number should be quoted together with the details and height of lettering required. In both cases, the approximate superficial area of the sign and details of the location, posts, mounting height and foundations should be given.

Section 13: Piling for Structures

Item	Root Narratives	Unit
	Piling Plant	
1	Establishment of piling plant for **FA**.	Item
2	Moving piling plant for **FA**.	No
	Precast Concrete Piles	
3	**JB** precast concrete pile **NCA**.	lin m
4	Driving **DJB** precast concrete pile **CA**.	lin m
5	Lengthening **DJB** precast concrete pile **NCA**.	lin m
6	Driving lengthened **DJB** precast concrete pile **CA**.	lin m
7	Stripping **DJB** precast concrete pile head **A**.	No
	Cast-in-Place Piles	
8	**DE** diameter cast-in-place pile shaft **NCA**.	lin m
9	**DE** diameter empty bore **A**.	lin m
10	Enlarged base to **E** diameter cast-in-place pile shaft **A**.	No
	Reinforcement for Cast-in-Place Piles	
11	**G** steel bar reinforcement nominal size **H** of 12 metre length or less.	tonne
12	**G** steel bar reinforcement nominal size **H** exceeding **I** in length but not exceeding **I**.	tonne
13	**G** steel helical reinforcement nominal size **H**.	tonne
	Steel Sheet Piles	
14	**J** steel sheet piling **KCL**.	sq m
15	**J** steel sheet piling lengthening piece **KCL**.	sq m
16	Extra over **J** steel sheet piling **KCL** for **MJ**.	lin m
17	Extra over **J** steel sheet piling lengthening piece **KCL** for **MJ**.	lin m
18	Driving **J** steel sheet piling **KCL**.	sq m
19	Driving lengthened **J** steel sheet piling **KCL**.	sq m
20	Extra over driving **J** steel sheet piling **KCL** for driving **MJ**.	lin m
21	Extra over driving lengthened **J** steel sheet sheet piling **KCL** for driving **MJ**.	lin m
22	Welding on lengthening piece to **J** steel sheet piling **KL**.	lin m

Item	Root Narratives	Unit
23	Cutting or burning off surplus length of *J* steel piling *KL*.	lin m
24	*J* walings.	tonne
25	*J* tie rods.	tonne
	Steel Bearing Piles	
26	*J* steel bearing pile *CA*.	lin m
27	*J* lengthening piece for steel bearing pile *CA*.	lin m
28	Driving *DJ* steel bearing pile *CA*.	lin m
29	Driving lengthened *DJ* steel bearing pile *CA*.	lin m
30	Welding on lengthening piece to *DJ* steel bearing pile *A*.	No
31	Cutting or burning off surplus length of *DJ* steel bearing pile *A*.	No

Group	Variables		
A	*1*	=	in trial piling as a separate operation in advance of the main piling
	2	=	in main piling
B	*1*	=	300 mm × 300 mm
	2	=	350 mm × 350 mm
	3	=	400 mm × 400 mm
	4	=	450 mm × 450 mm
	5	=	500 mm × 500 mm
	6	=	550 mm × 550 mm
	7	=	600 mm × 600 mm
C	*1*	=	not exceeding 5 metres in length
	2	=	exceeding 5 metres in length but not exceeding 10 metres
	3	=	exceeding 10 metres in length but not exceeding 15 metres
	4	=	exceeding 15 metres in length but not exceeding 20 metres and so on in steps of 5 metres
D	*1*	=	vertical
	2	=	raking
E	*1*	=	300 mm
	2	=	350 mm
	3	=	400 mm
	4	=	450 mm
	5	=	500 mm
	6	=	550 mm
	7	=	600 mm
	8	=	750 mm

Group	Variables		
E contd	*9*	=	900 mm
	10	=	1050 mm
	11	=	1200 mm
	12	=	1350 mm
	13	=	1500 mm
F	*1*	=	precast concrete piles
	2	=	cast-in-place piles
	3	=	steel sheet piles
	4	=	steel bearing piles
G	*1*	=	mild
	2	=	high yield
	3	=	stainless
H	*1*	=	16 mm and under
	2	=	20 mm and over
I	*1*	=	12 metres
	2	=	13·5 metres
	3 etc =		15 metres and so on in steps of 1·5 metres
J	*0*	=	No entry
	1 etc =		type [Engineers or Proprietary type reference]
K	*0*	=	No entry
	1	=	section modulus not exceeding 500 cm³/m
	2 etc =		section modulus exceeding 500 cm³/m but not exceeding 650 cm³/m and so in steps of 150 cm³/m

NB Variable *K* should not be used if Engineers or Proprietary type reference in variable *J* is used.

L	*1*	=	in main construction
	2	=	in anchorages
M	*1*	=	corner pile
	2	=	junction pile
	3	=	closure pile
	4	=	taper pile
	5 etc =		[Engineers reference for other special piles]
N	*0*	=	No entry
	1	=	[Engineers requirement for specific cement]

Notes

General

1 Attention is drawn to paragraphs 9, 21, 31 and 45 of the MMRB in which the commencement levels for the measure-

ment of driving and boring are defined. Should the Engineer wish to specify other commencement levels, such levels should be clearly shown in the tender documents.

Pre-boring or jetting is included in the Item coverage for driving precast concrete piles, cast-in-place pile shafts and steel bearing piles; this item provides for the operations to be undertaken either at the Contractor's choice (if permitted by the Engineer) or, alternatively, in conformity with the express requirements of the Specification. If, in the absence of any provision in the Specification, the Engineer requires this to be undertaken it would constitute a variation and would need to be dealt with accordingly.

Precast Concrete Piles

2 Reinforcement for precast concrete piling should not be separately measured but a separate bar bending schedule should be prepared for each pile which should state the total weight of reinforcement contained therein.

Cast-in Place Piles

3 Where the ground conditions are such that there is a possibility that casings for cast-in place piles will need to be left in, provisional sums should be included to cover the possibility.

Paragraph 24(h) of the MMRB requires the Contractor to cover 'taking measures required because of the presence of water in the bore or drive'. It is to be assumed that information available from soil surveys etc will be available to tenderers and that any special requirements or restrictions will have been specified. Beyond that, the measures which a Contractor can reasonably be expected to take must be considered in relation to Clause 12 of the ICE Conditions of Contract 5th Edition.

It will be noticed that the rates for cast-in place pile shafts include for providing apparatus for the inspection of pile bores. Where the Engineer has specific requirements in this respect, these shall be stated in the Contract. Requirements for specialist apparatus, however, such as closed circuit television, should not be treated in this way but should be arranged separately with a specialist firm. This could be done through the main contractor, in which case the measurement and payment should be covered by a 'Provisional Sum' included in the bill for this purpose.

Reinforcement for Cast-in Place Piles

4 The quantities of bar reinforcement should be given to three places of decimals.

Separate reinforcement schedules should be provided for each pile either on the Drawings or on bar bending schedules included in the Contract documents; these should show the complete dimensions and weights of all bars together with the laps required.

Steel Sheet Piles

5 The quantities of walings and ties should be given to three places of decimals.

Section 14: Formwork for Structures

Item	Root Narratives	Unit
	Formwork	
1	Formwork more than 300 mm wide *BAE*.	sq m
2	Formwork 300 mm wide or less at any inclination *AE*.	sq m
3	Formwork curved of both girth and width more than 300 mm at any inclination *AE*.	sq m
4	Formwork curved of girth or width of 300 mm or less at any inclination *AE*.	sq m
5	Formwork domed *AE*.	sq m
6	*F* void formers *D*.	lin m
	Patterned Profile Formwork	
7	Patterned profile formwork *BC*.	sq m
8	Patterned profile formwork curved at any inclination *C*.	sq m

Group	Variables		
A	*0*	=	No entry
	1	=	Class F1
	2	=	Class F2
	3	=	Class F3
	4	=	Class F4
	5 etc =		Class [other classes of finish]
B	*1*	=	horizontal or at any inclination up to and including 5° to the horizontal
	2	=	at any inclination more than 5° up to and including 85° to the horizontal
	3	=	at any inclination more than 85° up to and including 90° to the horizontal
C	*1* etc =		[Engineers type and finish reference]
D	*1* etc =		[unique dimensions as required]
E	*0*	=	No entry
	1	=	left in place

Group	Variables
F	**1** = Plastic
	2 = Expanded polystyrene
	3 = Metal core
	4 etc = [other named material]

Notes

General   1 The types of formed finish required should be shown on the Drawings. This is most satisfactorily dealt with by including a schedule with supporting diagrams on which the various faces are given lettered references for clear identification in the schedule. These schedules should also combine the uniformed finish requirements.

Although the areas requiring unformed finishes are not measured separately since they are covered by the Item coverage in Section 16, they should nevertheless be designated and defined in the schedule of finishes.

Where trial formwork panels are required, these can be combined with practical tests of concrete mixes. (See notes on Section 27).

Bill items for Patterned Profile Formwork should be allocated an Engineers type reference which identies the dimensions of the profile together with the finishes required to all the faces. Treatment to Concrete Faces after the Stocking of Formwork should be measured separately in Section 16: Concrete for Structures even though it may form part of the Engineers type reference.

Section 15: Steel Reinforcement for Structures

Item	Root Narratives	Unit
1	*A* steel bar reinforcement nominal size *B* of 12 m length or less *D*.	tonne
2	*A* steel bar reinforcement nominal size *B* exceeding *C* in length but not exceeding *CD*.	tonne
3	Fabric reinforcement BS Reference *E*.	sq m
4	*A* steel helical reinforcement nominal size *B*.	tonne
5	*A* steel dowel *F*.	No

Group	Variables		
A	1	=	Mild
	2	=	High yield
	3	=	Stainless
B	1	=	16 mm and under
	2	=	20 mm and over
C	1	=	12 metres
	2	=	13·5 metres
	3 etc =		15·0 metres and so on in steps of 1·5 metres
D	0	=	No entry
	1	=	threaded through holes in members
E	1	=	A393
	2	=	A252
	3	=	A193
	4	=	A142
	5	=	A98
	6	=	B1131
	7	=	B785
	8	=	B503
	9	=	B385
	10	=	B283
	11	=	B196
	12	=	C785
	13	=	C503
	14	=	C385
	15	=	C283

Group	Variables
E contd	**16** = D98
	17 = D49
F	**1** etc = [diameter and length]

Notes

General

1 The quantities of bar reinforcement should be given to three places of decimals.

Separate reinforcement schedules should be provided for each structural element either on the Drawings or on bar bending schedules included in the Contract documents; these should show the complete dimensions and weights of all bars and fabric together with the laps required.

Where the Engineer has particular requirements on the threading of reinforcement through holes in members, these should be stated on the Drawings together with details of bar splicing and coupling.

Reinforcement for precast concrete members or units should not be separately measured but a separate bar bending schedule should be prepared for each member or unit which should state the total weight of reinforcement contained therein. Consideration should be given to any alternative reinforcement arrangements suggested either at tender stage or during the course of the Contract by the Contractor or his Supplier.

Section 16: Concrete for Structures

Item	Root Narratives	Unit
	In Situ Concrete	
1	In situ concrete class *ABC*.	cu m
	Precast Members	
2	Precast *DEFM*	No
	G m long	
	H cu m volume	
	I tonnes weight	
3	Precast *KFM*.	No
4	Precast *LFM*.	lin m
5	Precast culvert *JM*.	lin m
	Treatment to Concrete Faces after the Striking of Formwork	
6	*N* treatment to concrete faces after the striking of formwork.	sq m

Group	Variables		
A	*1*	=	E
	2	=	52·5/37·5
	3	=	52·5/20
	4	=	52·5/10
	5	=	45/37·5
	6	=	45/20
	7	=	45/10
	8	=	37·5/37·5
	9	=	37·5/20
	10	=	37·5/10
	11	=	30/37·5
	12	=	30/20
	13	=	30/10
	14	=	22·5/37·5
	15	=	22·5/20
B	*0*	=	No entry (implies ordinary Portland or Portland blast furnace cement)
	1	=	with rapid hardening cement
	2	=	with sulphate resisting cement
	3	=	with supersulphated cement
	4	=	with white cement
	5	=	with coloured cement (colour stated)

Group	Variables		
C	0	=	No entry
	1	=	in blinding 75 mm or less in thickness
D	1	=	reinforced
	2	=	pretensioned prestressed
	3	=	post-tensioned prestressed
E	1	=	member
	2	=	slab
	3	=	segmental unit
F	1 etc =		[Engineers mark references]
G	1 etc =		[unique length as required]
H	1 etc =		[unique volume as required]
I	1 etc =		[unique weight as required]
J	1 etc =		[Engineers reference for type/size]
K	1	=	hinge
	2	=	specially moulded block
L	1	=	coping
	2	=	plinth
M	0	=	No entry
	1	=	curved
N	1	=	Bush hammering
	2	=	Exposed aggregate
	3	=	Knocked rib
	4 etc =		[other stated treatments]

Notes

General

1 For testing of in situ concrete and precast members see Section 27.

In situ Concrete

2 Since itemisation within each structural element is related principally to concrete strength and aggregate size, the Drawings should show directly or in schedule form where the different classes of concrete are required in each structural element.

Precast Members

3 Where precast concrete construction is involved, a schedule of precast members and units should be included on the Drawings summarising unit Mark reference, numbers, dimensions, construction data, and location in the structure.

In situ concrete infilling between adjacent precast members should be separately measured where the width at any point in the cavity to be filled is 100 mm or more. Infilling to cavities of less than 100 mm width is included in Item coverage.

If precast members have to incorporate bearing components supplied as proprietary articles by a separate specialist manufacturer (eg the top plates of roller bearings), then the Drawings should indicate that the components are to be supplied by others but incorporated by the beam manufacturer. Precast reinforced, precast pretensioned and post-tensioned prestressed members are covered under Precast Members in this section. Any subsequent in situ post-tensioning of members in the construction should be measured in accordance with Section 17. All information with regard to the positioning of tendon ducts etc necessary for the post-tensioning should however be shown on the Drawings to facilitate the pricing of the appropriate precast members.

For precast pretensioned members, the prestressing force at critical points and eccentricity to be provided at release should be stated so that specialist manufacturers may offer alternative forms or positions of tendons which best suit their processes. This information should be given as part of the schedule of reinforcement for each member.

Treatment to Concrete Faces After the Striking of the Formwork

4 Treatment to concrete faces after the striking of formwork is only intended to cover formed finishes on the face of the concrete such as bush hammering, exposed aggregate etc. Applied finishes such as brickwork, masonry, cast blockwork and the like should be measured in accordance with Sections 24 and 25 as appropriate.

Section 17: In Situ Post-tensioned Prestressing for Structures

Item	Root Narratives	Unit
1	*A* prestressing tendon *DBC* metres long.	No
2	Stressing and grouting internal *A* tendon *DBC* metres long.	No
3	Stressing external *A* tendon *DBC* metres long.	No
4	Final stressing and grouting tendon *DBC* metres long in precast member supplied partially prestressed.	No
5	Protective covering to *A* external tendon *DBC* metres long.	No

Group	Variables		
A	*1*	=	longitudinal
	2	=	transverse
	3 etc =		[unique directions defined by Engineer]
B	*1* etc =		[Engineers type references]
C	*1* etc =		[differing stated lengths]
D	*1*	=	for in situ concrete construction
	2	=	for segmental construction

In situ Post-tensioned Prestressing for Structures

Notes

1 Measurement of tendons by numbers make it imperative that the composition of the various types and sizes of tendon are fully defined and scheduled on the Drawings. These should therefore, show tendon reference numbers, outline profiles, lengths, locations in the structure, composition, anchorage and tension requirements, and the order in which the tendons are to be stressed.

The grouping into one item of tendons which differ only in respect of length within a limit of ± 5% of a stated length is intended to cover the emergence of otherwise identical tendons at different anchorage points eg straight and catenary tendons or staggered anchorages in the surface or soffit of a superstructure.

Section 18: Steelwork for Structures

Item	Root Narratives	Unit
	Fabrication of Steelwork	
1	Fabrication of *ABCDE*.	tonne
	Erection of Steelwork	
2	Trial erection of steelwork at the place of fabrication.	Item
3	Permanent erection of *F* steelwork.	tonne
	Corrugated Steel Structures	
4	Corrugated steel *GHIJK* metres in length.	No

Group	Variables		
A	*1*	=	main members
	2	=	deck panels
	3	=	subsidiary steelwork
B	*1*	=	comprising rolled sections
	2	=	comprising plated rolled sections
	3	=	comprising plated girders
	4	=	comprising box girders
C	*0*	=	No entry
	1 etc =		[Engineers mark references for different combinations of steel grades]
D	*0*	=	No entry
	1	=	in curved section
E	*0*	=	No entry
	1	=	in tapering section
F	*1*	=	substructure
	2	=	superstructure
G	*1*	=	pipe
	2	=	pipe-arch
	3	=	underpass
	4	=	arch
H	*1* etc =		[Engineers type reference]

Group	Variables
I	*1* etc = [unique span or diameter as required]
J	*1* etc = [unique thickness of plate as required]
K	*1* etc = [unique length as required]

Notes

General
1 The quantities of steelwork should be given to three places of decimals.
For welding procedure trials and flame cutting procedure trials see Section 27.

Fabrication
2 The fabrication itemisation features for main members, deck panels and subsidiary steelwork must all be identifiable from the Drawings; this should be achieved by a combination of appropriate titling and/or scheduling of the steelwork details; the provision of separate Drawings for the main members and deck panels would be an aid to clarity. The Drawings and schedules should also show the various combinations of grades of steel required for each member, together with requirements in respect of rivets, bolts, nuts and washers, and any integral components measured with each, eg bearing plates welded on.

Permanent Erection
3 Permanent erection of main members, deck panels and subsidiary steelwork is to be taken as a single items except where different forms of constructions are involved as, for example, would be the case with composite beam and slab approach spans to a bow string centre span.

Section 19: Protection of Steelwork against Corrosion

Item	Root Narratives	Unit
1	Protective system **A**.	sq m
2	Desiccant.	kg
3	Vapour phase inhibitor.	kg

Group	Variables
A	*1* etc = [Engineers reference]

Notes

General   **1** The protective systems should be described in Specification clause 1910 together with the additional information which the Tenderers will require to complete Form BES/P2.

Section 20: Waterproofing for Structures

Item	Root Narratives	Unit
1	*A* waterproofing system on surfaces *BC*.	sq m
2	*A* waterproofing system on domed surfaces.	sq m
3	*DE* sprayed or brushed on as waterproofing to surfaces of any width and at any inclination.	sq m

Group	Variables		
A	*1*	=	Mastic asphalt
	2	=	Prefabricated sheeting
	3	=	Rubberised filled bitumen
B	*1*	=	more than 300 mm wide
	2	=	300 mm wide or less at any inclination
C	*0*	=	No entry
	1	=	horizontal or at any inclination up to and including 45° to the horizontal
	2	=	at any inclination more than 45° up to and including 90° to the horizontal
D	*1*	=	One coat
	2	=	Two coats
	3	=	Three coats
E	*1*	=	of tar
	2	=	of bitumen

Notes

General

1 The area of the Waterproofing System should be detailed on the Drawings together with details of any special treatments at copings, service ducts, membrane edges, joints and junctions between different planes. Where the System requires a protective layer details of this should also be given.

Section 21: Bridge Bearings

Item	Root Narratives	Unit
1	Supply **AB** bearing.	No
2	Installation of **AB** bearing.	No

Group	Variables	
A	**1** etc =	[Engineers type reference]
B	**0** =	No entry
	1 etc =	[size of bearing where not covered by type reference]

Notes

General 1 Each type and size of bearing should be fully described on the Drawings and be given an identification reference number. For testing of bearings see Section 27.

Section 22: Metal Parapets

Item	Root Narratives	Unit
1	*A* Group P1 parapet *B* high comprising *CDE*.	lin m
2	*A* Group P2 parapet *B* high comprising *CDFG*.	lin m
3	*A* Group P4 parapet *B* high *H*	lin m
4	*A* Group P5 parapet *B* high comprising *CG*.	lin m
5	*A* Group P5 parapet *B* high *H*.	lin m

Group	Variables		
A	*1*	=	Fabrication of
	2	=	Installation of
B	*0*	=	No entry
	1 etc =		[unique height as required]
C	*0*	=	No entry
	1	=	aluminium frangible posts and aluminium horizontal rails
	2	=	steel yielding posts and steel horizontal rails
	3	=	aluminium yielding/frangible post and aluminium horizontal rails
	4 etc =		[Engineers reference]
D	*0*	=	No entry
	1	=	steel hydrafence
E	*0*	=	No entry
	1	=	steel hydraulic posts and steel horizontal rails
	2	=	concrete plinth, steel horizontal rails and energy absorbing brackets
	3	=	splayed concrete plinth, steel posts and steel horizontal rails
	4	=	splayed concrete plinth, aluminium posts and aluminium horizontal rails
	5	=	aluminium frangible posts and steel horizontal rails
	6	=	steel yielding posts, steel horizontal rails and energy absorbing brackets
F	*0*	=	No entry
	1	=	steel hydraulic posts and steel horizontal rails and handrail
	2	=	steel yielding posts and steel hollow section vertical infill

Group	Variables
G	*0* = No entry *1* = with mesh infill *2* etc = [Engineers reference for solid infill]
H	*1* etc = [Engineers reference for Group 4 and 5 parapets]

Notes

General   1 The item library covers the approved highway bridge parapets within the various groups described in Technical Memorandum Number BE5. Full details of these parapets should be given on the Drawings including such information as the height and type of mesh or other filling, details of the connections, fastenings, holding-down bolts, sockets for baseplates, anchorage assemblies and casting in requirements.

The protective system required on parapets should be described in Clause 1910 together with the additional information which the Tenderers will require to complete Form BES/92.

Section 23: Movement Joints for Structures

Item	Root Narratives	Unit
	Movement Joints to Bridge and Viaduct Decks	
1	*A* joint *B* with *C* mm gap width and *D* metres in length.	No
2	Hinge throat *B* perimeter *D* metres.	No
	Movement Joints other than to Bridge and Decks	
3	Viaduct *E* joint filler *C* mm thick.	
4	*F* joint sealant *C* mm × *C* mm.	lin m
5	*G* water bar *C* mm × *C* mm.	lin m
6	*G* water stop *C* mm × *C* mm	lin m

Group	Variables		
A	*1*	=	Expansion
	2	=	Fixed
	3	=	Contraction
B	*1* etc =		[Engineers type references]
C	*1* etc =		[unique dimensions as required]
D	*1* etc =		[unique length or perimeter as required]
E	*1*	=	Fibreboard
	2	=	Expanded synthetic rubber
	3	=	Expanded polyethylene
	4 etc =		[Engineers particular description)
F	*1*	=	Hot-poured
	2	=	Cold-poured
	3	=	Preformed compression
	4 etc =		[Engineers particular description]
G	1 etc =		[Engineers reference]

Notes

General 1 In order to present the Contractor with information in a form which will facilitate the building-up of a price, a comprehensive list of the components required for the movement joint should be included in a schedule on the Drawings. These components should be quantified in convenient units and items affecting the structure (formwork, grooves, mortar beds and the like) kept separate from the 'specialist' items for which the Contractor will probably need to obtain quotations. In the case of an expansion joint to a bridge deck, the expansion joint for footpaths and verges are often different from the joint for the carriageway; where the different joints are measured separately the Drawings should show clearly which components are to be included with each respective joint.

The preceding note should not however preclude the whole expansion joint, from parapet to parapet, being measured as one complete type of expansion joint where the Engineer considers it appropriate to do so. When it is measured in this way each complete joint should be given a mark reference number and be fully detailed and described on the Drawings.

Movement Joints

2 The Drawings should separately identify movement joints and construction joints as formwork and water bars for construction joints are included in the item coverage in Section 16 Concrete for Structures, but movement joints and associated formwork are measured separately.

Section 24: Brickwork for Structures

Item	Root Narratives	Unit
1	Brickwork in **AB** bricks **C** thick **DEFG**.	sq m
2	Extra over **A** brickwork **D** for **B** bricks.	sq m
3	Brickwork in **AB** bricks **C** thick **DEFG**.	Item

Group	Variables	
A	**0** =	No entry
	1 =	Common
	2 =	Engineering
	3 =	Engineering Class A
	4 =	Engineering Class B
	5 etc =	[Engineers reference for type of common or engineering brick]
B	**0** =	No entry
	1 =	facing
	2 etc =	[Engineers reference for type of facing brick]
C	**1** =	half brick
	2 =	one brick
	3 =	one and a half brick
	4 =	two brick
	5 =	two and a half brick
	6 =	three brick
D	**0** =	No entry
	1 =	in stretcher bond
	2 =	in Flemish bond
	3 =	in English bond
	4 etc =	[Engineers reference for other bonds]
E	**0** =	No entry
	1 =	curved on plan
F	**0** =	No entry
	1 =	with a battered face
G	**1** =	in walls
	2 =	in facework to concrete
	3 =	in arches
	4 =	in alteration work

General

Notes

1 Full details of the types and classes of bricks required should be shown on the Drawings with any particular requirements for jointing, bonding, facing, pointing, tying and reinforcing.

Section 25: Masonry for Structures

Item	Root Narratives	Unit
1	Masonry *ABCDE*.	cu m
2	Masonry *ABCDE*.	Item
3	*A* coping with a cross section *F* sq mm *C*.	lin m
4	*A* specially shaped and dressed string course with a cross section *F* sq mm *C*.	lin m
5	Masonry *GH*.	No

Group	Variables	
A	*0* =	No entry
	1 etc =	[Engineers material type reference]
B	*0* =	No entry
	1 etc =	[Engineers reference for coursing]
C	*0* =	No entry
	1 =	curved on plan
D	*0* =	No entry
	1 =	with a battered face
E	*1* =	in walls
	2 =	in facework to concrete
	3 =	in arches
	4 =	in alteration work
F	*1* etc =	[unique dimensions as required]
G	*1* =	block
	2 =	feature
	3 =	stone
H	*1* etc =	[Engineers mark reference]

Section 26: is not taken up

Section 27: Testing

Item	Root Narratives	Unit
	Pile Testing	
1	Establishment of pile testing equipment for **AB**	Item
2	Load testing of **AB** to **CD**.	No
	Practical Tests of Concrete for Structures	
3	Concrete test **EF**.	No
	Testing Precast Concrete Member for Structures	
4	Load test **GH** with **C** point load.	No
5	Load test **GH** to destruction.	No
	Grouting Trials	
6	Grouting trial **IJ**.	No
	Welding and Flame Cutting Procedure Trails	
7	**K** procedure trail at the place of fabrication.	Item
	Test of Bearings	
8	**L** of **MN** bearing.	No

Group	Variables		
A	1	=	precast concrete piles
	2	=	cast-in-place piles
	3	=	steel bearing piles
B	1	=	in trial piling as a separate operation in advance of the main piling
	2	=	in main piling
C	1 etc =		[value of test load to be stated in tonnes]
D	0	=	No entry
	1 etc =		at an angle of [ ]°
E	0	=	No entry
	1 etc =		mould type [ ]
F	0	=	No entry
	1 etc =		reinforcement type [ ]

Group	Variables		
G	*1*	=	member
	2	=	slab
	3	=	unit
H	*1* etc =		[Engineers design reference]
I	*0*	=	No entry
	1 etc =		duct diameter [　] mm
J	*0*	=	No entry
	1 etc =		configuration type [　]
K	*1*	=	Welding
	2	=	Flame cutting
L	*1*	=	Compression test
	2	=	Shear test
	3	=	Bond test
	4	=	Test for physical properties
	5	=	Weathering test
M	*1* etc =		[Engineers type reference]
N	*0*	=	No entry
	1 etc =		[size of bearing where not covered by type reference]

Notes

General

1 The Specification and MMRB have been drawn up in accordance with Departmental policy which requires that the testing of materials and workmanship, other than for production testing of coupon plates from welded details, should be carried out by the Engineer in his own laboratory on Site or otherwise under the Engineer's direction. The Site laboratory may or may not be erected and equipped by the Contractor under the terms of the Contract, but other than this the Contractor takes no part in compliance testing beyond providing the samples for testing, and general assistance to the Engineer upon request. The Contractor will, however, be required to carry out performance tests, eg pile and beam loading tests, and the items for such tests should be provided in the appropriate structural element section of the Bill.

As the number of tests and trials required cannot be predetermined, items under this Section should normally be classified as 'Provisional'.

Where the Engineer requires the Contractor to arrange testing at any place other than the Site or the place of manufacture or fabrication of the materials tested this should be described in the Contract in sufficient detail to enable the Contractor to price or allow for same in his Tender.

Piling

2 Pile tests being performance tests, should be billed in the Piling Section of the Bill of Quantities. Full details of the test loads required and settlement criteria should be given on the Drawings.

The Specification NFG Clause 2720.5 states that additional or substitute clauses will be required should the Engineer wish to determine the ultimate capacity of a pile. In such a case the additional or substitute clause should be examined to assess its effect on the MMRB and any necessary modifications should be made.

Concrete

3 Trial mixes required for the design of concrete mixes are included in the rates for concrete. It may, however, be necessary to carry out practical tests to check the suitability of the mix for compaction around reinforcement and, when combined with trial formwork panels, to check the surface finish; these tests should be fully described and detailed showing the dimensions required and itemised in this Section of the Bill.

Testing Precast Concrete Members for Structures

4 Ultra Sonic and Radiographic testing will normally be carried out by a specialist firm appointed by and reporting directly to the Engineer and does not normally form part of the Contract.

Grouting Trials

5 Grouting trials carried out in respect of prestressing ducts should be billed under the 'Testing' Section of the Bill and full details of the requirements for each trial should be given on the Drawings.

Welding and Flamecutting Procedure Trials

6 Procedure trials for welding and flame cutting should be billed under the appropriate structure construction heading.

Tests of Bearings

7 The testing of bearings is intended only to act as a control of production. They should be billed under the appropriate structure construction heading.

Section 28: is not taken up

Section 29: Accommodation Works and Works for Statutory Undertakers

General

Notes

1 Where Accommodation Works and Works for Statutory Undertakers are known prior to tendering they should be billed in accordance with the various Sections of the MMRB or if more appropriate, and subject to the Engineers discretion, as a measured lump sum item.

Alternatively where the extent of any Accommodation Works and Works for Statutory Undertakers is envisaged but not known in sufficient detail to include as billed items then a Provisional Sum should be included in the Bill of Quantities.

Section 30: Provisional Sums and Prime Cost Items

Item	Root Narratives	Unit
1	Allow the Provisional Sum of £............	
	for *A* to be executed by the Main Contractor.	Sum
2	Allow the *B* of £............ for *C* to be	
	executed by a firm nominated by the Engineer.	Sum
	Add for labours	Lump Sum
	Add for all other charges and profit	%
3	Allow the *B* of £............ for *D* to be	
	supplied by a firm nominated by the Engineer	Sum
	Add for labours	Lump Sum
	Add for all other charges and profit	%
	Installation of goods or materials into the	
	Works	Measurement Item as necessary

Group	Variables	
A	*1* etc =	[Engineers description of the Work to be executed and goods, materials or services to be supplied]
B	*1* =	Provisional Sum
	2 =	Prime Cost (PC) Item
C	*1* etc =	[Engineers description of the work to be executed]
D	*1* etc =	[Engineers description of the goods, materials or services to be supplied]

Notes

General

1 A preamble to the Bill of Quantities may have to be inserted to cover the measurement of installation of goods and materials, other than Bridge Bearings and Metal Parapets, supplied by a firm nominated by the Engineer.

The term 'labours' is defined in MMRB Part III, Preambles to Bill of Quantities in Preamble 6 sideheaded Labours.

If the Engineer has doubts, on whether certain works to be executed or goods materials or services to be supplied will be required at all, then use should be made of a Provisional Sum rather than a Prime Cost Item.

PART C

Notes, Methods of Measurement and Library of Standard Item Descriptions for Work not Specified in the Specification for Road and Bridge Works

Special Note

The several measurement items given in the following pages are for work not specified in the Specification for Road and Bridge Works but which are often required for Highway Contracts. The Units, Measurement Notes and Itemisation will suffice in most cases, but the Item coverage, because of the lack of standard specification covering these works, must be checked against the particular specification and drawings and modified as necessary to conform with the requirements of the particular specification and drawings.

Any measurement item contained herein or amended to suit the particular specification and drawings shall be written into the Contract by means of an additional Preamble (see Preamble 'Amendment to Method of Measurement').

In the following pages the paragraphs covering amendments to the MMRB (other than for Section 6: Earthworks) have been numbered sequentially within each Section. When these amendments are incorporated into the Preambles of the Bill of Quantities the paragraphs should be renumbered so that they are numbered sequentially to last paragraph number of the appropriate MMRB Section. In the case of Section 6 the paragraph numbering used in these amendments is covered in the Notes to that Section.

Section 1: Preliminaries

Notes

Modifications to Principal Offices for the Engineer

1 The full extent of the modifications should be clearly shown at tender stage to enable the Contractor to allow in the rates and prices for such modifications.

It is envisaged that only one modification would be required to the offices. Where more than one is however required, the extent and timing of each modification should be shown in the Contract and separately identified and measured in the Bill of Quantities.

Only one item should be billed for 'Dismantling of principal offices for the Engineer' which in the above case will be for the dismantling of the modified accommodation.

Scheme Signboard

2 Details of scheme signboards should be specified in the Contract and include such information regarding their location, size, amount and type of lettering or wording, reflectorisation and illumination if required and the period of time required to be erected. Each signboard should be cross referenced to the bill item by a type letter or number.

Radio Communication System

3 Details of the radio communication system should be specified in the Contract and include information regarding the type and extent of the system and the period of time required on Site.

Modifications to Principal Offices for the Engineer

Units

1 The units of measurement shall be:
    (i) modifications to principal offices for the Engineer
    .... item

Measurement

2 Measurement shall be for the modifications stated in the Contract as being required by the Engineer.

Itemisation

3 Separate items shall be provided for modifications to principal offices for the Engineer in accordance with Part II paragraphs 3 and 4 and the following:

Group	Feature
I	1 Modifications to principal offices for the Engineer.

Modifications to Principal Offices for the Engineer
Item coverage

4 *The items for modifications to principal offices for the Engineer shall in accordance with the Preambles to Bill of Quantities General Directions include for:*
(a) *temporary dismantling, re-erection and re-establishment of offices to suit modified layouts;*
(b) *modifications to water, sanitation, heating, power and lighting services, fences, notice and direction boards, vehicle access, hardstandings, parking areas, footpaths, office equipment, furnishings, fittings, supplies and telephones;*
(c) *receiving back from the Engineer and removing surplus equipment, furniture, fittings and supplies off Site;*
(d) *disposal of surplus material;*
(e) *reinstatement of the sites occupied by temporary accommodation;*
(f) *credit value of surplus equipment or material which becomes the property of the Contractor and transport and delivery to the Employer of equipment or material which becomes the property of the Employer.*

Scheme Signboard

Units

5 The units of measurement shall be:
(i) scheme signboard...................number.

Itemisation

6 Separate items shall be provided for scheme signboard in accordance with Part II paragraphs 3 and 4 and the following:

Group	Feature
I	1 Scheme signboard.
II	2 Different types.

Scheme Signboard

Item coverage

7 *The items for scheme signboard shall in accordance with the Preambles to Bill of Quantities General Directions include for:*
(a) *excavation in any material including rock and reinforced concrete and loading into transport, upholding the sides and keeping the earthworks free of water;*
(b) *backfilling and compaction;*
(c) *supports;*
(d) *formwork (as Section 14 paragraph 4);*
(f) *in situ concrete (as Section 16 paragraph 4);*
(g) *disposal of surplus material;*
(h) *painting, reflectorisation and illumination;*
(i) *cleaning, maintaining and repairing;*
(j) *dismantling and removing from Site;*
(k) *unless otherwise stated in the Contract, reinstatement of surfaces.*

Units

Radio Communication System for the Engineer
8 The units of measurement shall be:
(i) radio communication system the Engineer........item.

Itemisation

9 Separate items shall be provided for radio communication system for the Engineer in accordance with Part II paragraphs 3 and 4 and the following:

Group	Feature
I	1 Radio communication system for the Engineer.

Radio Communication System for the Engineer

Item coverage

10 *The items for radio communication system for the Engineer shall in accordance with the Preambles to Bill of Quantities General Directions include for:*
(*a*) *arranging with Post Office Corporation for licences, wavelengths and channels and costs arising therefrom;*
(*b*) *equipment and installation;*
(*c*) *rental, running costs and charges for power;*
(*d*) *depreciation, maintenance and repairs;*
(*e*) *replacement equipment when the regular equipment is unavailable or unserviceable for more than 24 hours;*
(*f*) *receiving back from the Engineer and removing equipment and supplies off Site.*

Item	Root Narratives	Unit
	Modifications to Principal Office for the Engineer	
1	Modifications to principal offices for the Engineer.	Item
	Scheme Signboard	
2	Scheme signboard *A*.	No
	Radio Communication System for the Engineer	
3	Radio communication system for the Engineer.	Item

Group	Variables
A	*1* etc = [Engineers reference by type, letter or number]

Section 2: Site Clearance

General

Notes

1 Whilst the recovery of existing items and materials is generally uneconomical, there are occasions when this is required particularly when they are not the property of the Employer. In such cases, these items and materials should be identified on the Drawings and itemised in the Bill of Quantities with the location of the store off Site or full details of new foundations and bases where required for relaying or re-erecting stated in the Contract. (For relaying or re-erecting items taken up or down in this Section, see relevant Sections hereof).

Take Up or Down and Set Aside or Remove to Store off Site

Units

1 The units of measurement shall be:
Take up or down and set aside or remove to store off Site the following:
    (i) paved areas and the like............square metre.
   (ii) kerbing, channelling, edging, walls and the like...... linear metre.
  (iii) lamp standards, traffic signs, street furniture and the like...........number.

Itemisation

2 Separate items shall be provided for take up or down and set aside or remove to store off Site in accordance with Part II paragraphs 3 and 4 and the following:

Group	Feature
I	1 Take up or down and set aside. 2 Take up or down and remove to store off Site.
II	1 Paved areas and the like. 2 Kerbing, channelling, edging, walls and the like. 3 Lamp standards, traffic signs, street furniture and the like.
III	1 Different materials.

Take up or Down and Set Aside

3 *The items for take up or down and set aside shall in accordance with the Preambles to Bill of Quantities General Directions include for:*

Item coverage

(*a*) *breaking up foundations;*
(*b*) *cleaning, stacking, protecting and labelling;*
(*c*) *disconnecting and sealing services;*
(*d*) *backfilling with suitable material from any source and compaction;*
(*e*) *making good to severed ends of existing walls or fences;*
(*f*) *storage facilities;*
(*g*) *disposal of surplus material;*
(*h*) *replacing items damaged during the foregoing operations.*

Take Up or Down and Remove to Store Off Site Item coverage

4 *The items for take up or down and remove to store off Site shall in accordance with the Preambles to Bill of Quantities General Directions include for:*
(*a*) *breaking up foundations;*
(*b*) *cleaning, protecting and labelling;*
(*c*) *transporting to store off Site, nominated by the Engineer;*
(*d*) *unloading and stacking;*
(*e*) *disconnecting and sealing services;*
(*f*) *backfilling with suitable material from any source and compaction;*
(*g*) *making good to severed ends of existing walls or fences;*
(*h*) *disposal of surplus material;*
(*i*) *replacing items damaged during the foregoing operations.*

Item	Root Narratives	Unit
	Take Up or Down and Set Aside or Remove to Store Off Site	
1	Take up or down **AB**.	sq m
2	Take up or down **AC**.	lin m
3	Take up or down **ADEF**.	lin m
4	Take up or down **AGH**.	No

Group	Variables		
A	*1*	=	and set aside
	2	=	and remove to store off Site
B	*1*	=	precast concrete flags
	2	=	stone slab paving
	3	=	brick paving
	4	=	cobble paving
	5	=	granite sett paving
	6	=	block paving
	7 etc =		[other named material]

Group	Variables		
C	1	=	precast concrete kerbing
	2	=	stone kerbing
	3	=	granite kerbing
	4	=	precast concrete channelling
	5	=	precast concrete edging
	6 etc	=	[other named material]
D	1	=	half
	2	=	one
	3	=	one and a half
	4	=	two
	5	=	two and a half
	6	=	225 mm thick
	7	=	300 mm thick
	8	=	375 mm thick
	9	=	450 mm thick
	10	=	525 mm thick
	11	=	600 mm thick
E	1	=	brick wall
	2	=	uncoursed random rubble wall
	3	=	coursed random rubble wall
	4	=	random rubble brought to course wall
	5	=	dry stone wall
	6 etc	=	[other named material]
F	1	=	300 mm high
	2	=	375 mm high
	3	=	450 mm high
	4	=	525 mm high
	5	=	600 mm high
	6	=	675 mm high
	7	=	750 mm high
	8	=	825 mm high
	9	=	900 mm high
	10	=	975 mm high and so on in steps of 75 mm
G	1	=	bench seat
	2	=	cattle trough
	3	=	traffic bollard
	4	=	parking meter
	5	=	belisha, panda and zebra crossing lights
	6	=	traffic control signals
	7	=	lighting columns
	8	=	traffic sign
	9	=	traffic sign including posts
	10	=	internally illuminated traffic sign

Group	Variables		
G contd.	*11*	=	internally illuminated traffic sign including posts
	12	=	externally illuminated traffic sign
	13	=	externally illuminated traffic sign including posts
	14 etc =		[other named items]
H	*1* etc =		[Engineers reference]

Section 5: Drainage and Service Ducts

Raising or Lowering Covers and Gratings on Existing Chambers and Gullies

Units

1 The units of measurement shall be:
(i) raising the level, lowering the level.........number.

Itemisation

2 Separate items shall be provided for raising or lowering covers and gratings on existing chambers and gullies in accordance with Part II paragraphs 3 and 4 and the following:

Group	Feature
I	1 Raising the level. 2 Lowering the level.
II	1 Different sizes of cover. 2 Different sizes of grating.
III	1 Different types of cover. 2 Different types of grating.
IV	1 Different sizes of chamber. 2 Different sizes of gully.
V	1 Differing construction of chamber. 2 Differing construction of gully.
VI	1 150 mm or less. 2 Exceeding 150 mm but not exceeding 300 mm and so in stages of 150 mm.

Raising the Level
Lowering the Level

Item coverage

3 *The items for raising the level, lowering the level shall in accordance with the Preambles to Bill of Quantities General Directions include for:*
(a) *excavation in any material including rock and reinforced concrete and loading into transport, upholding the sides and keeping the earthworks free of water;*
(b) *taking precautions to avoid damage to sewers and drains;*
(c) *take up existing cover or grating including frame and clean and set aside for reuse;*
(d) *demolition and preparation to receive new construction;*
(e) *construction of walls, roof and cover slabs and shafts including in situ concrete (as Section 16 paragraph 4) surrounds and corbelling for cover and making good;*

(f) *step irons, safety chains, ladders, handholds and other fittings;*

(g) *bedding eixsting cover or grating including frame;*

(h) *formwork (as Section 14 paragraph 4);*

(i) *reinforcement (as Section 15 paragraph 5);*

(j) *backfilling with in situ concrete (as Section 16 paragraph 4) or suitable material from any source and compaction;*

(k) *disposal (as Section 6 paragraph 25) of unsuitable material and surplus suitable material.*

Item	Root Narratives	Unit
	Raising or Lowering Covers and Gratings on Existing Chambers and Gullies	
1	*A* the level of *BC* cover and frame on *BD* chamber by *E*.	No
2	*A* the level of *BF* grating and frame on *BG* gully by *E*.	No

Group	Variables		
A	*1*	=	Raising
	2	=	Lowering
B	*1* etc =		[unique size as required]
C	*1*	=	Grade A
	2	=	Grade B
	3 etc =		[Engineers type reference]
D	*1*	=	brick
	2	=	precast concrete
	3	=	in situ concrete
E	*1*	=	150 mm or less
	2 etc =		exceeding 150 mm but not exceeding 300 mm (and so in stages of 150 mm)
F	*1*	=	Grade D
	2	=	Grade E
	3 etc =		[Engineers type reference]
G	*1*	=	precast concrete
	2	=	salt glazed stoneware
	3	=	vitrified clay
	4	=	cast iron
	5	=	in situ concrete

Section 6: Earthworks

Landscape Areas and Noise Barrier Earth Mounds

Notes

1 In order to cover for the use of material in landscape areas and noise barrier earth mounds it is first necessary to amend some of the MMRB definitions and measurement clauses, and secondly to provide additional units, measurement itemisation and item coverage for the measurement of this work. The directional paragraphs numbered 1 to 8 inclusive in the following pages cover the amendments to the MMRB paragraphs deemed necessary for these additional items of work with the actual amended paragraphs indicated by a suffix (A). The paragraphs, covering the additional units, measurements itemisation and item coverage have been numbered sequentially following the last MMRB paragraph number in Section 6: Earthworks. These are identified following directional paragraph number 9.

2 For the purpose of this sub-section, it has been assumed that:

(a) Specification clause 601.1 (ii) has been amended in order to provide for the use of 'unsuitable material' in landscape areas and noise barrier earth mounds.

(b) The compaction required is more than that provided by the traversing of earth moving plant but different from that required for the compaction of embankments. Where the standard of compaction required is only that produced by the traversing of earth moving plant then the MMRB should be amended to state that compaction in these cases will not be measured.

(c) For economic reasons only material available from Site will be used in these works.

(d) Both landscape areas and noise barrier earth mounds are required in a particular contract. Where only one of these works is required in a particular contract then the following amending and additional paragraphs should be reworded by the deletion of the work not required.

Where landscape areas and noise barrier earth mounds are specified the following amendments are necessary to the paragraphs set out in Sections 5 and 6.

Section 5: Drainage and Service Ducts
1 Insert the following paragraph 1(A)
   1(A) Notwithstanding the provision of paragraph 1 of this Section the Earthworks Outline shall for landscape areas

and noise barrier earth mounds be the level of the ground immediately prior to the commencement of and covered by any work in these areas or on those mounds.

Section 6 : Earthworks

2 Insert the following as paragraph 3(A) ;

3(A) Notwithstanding the provisions of paragraph 3 of this Section where any settlement or penetration occurs in landscape areas and noise barrier earth mounds, then the additional deposition, fill and compaction required shall not be measured.

3 Insert the following as paragraph 5(A)

5(A) Notwithstanding the provisional of paragraph 5 of this Section the Earthworks Outline shall for landscape areas and noise barrier earth mounds be the level of the ground immediately prior to the commencement of and covered by any work in these areas or on these mounds.

4 Insert the following as additional sub paragraphs to paragraph 14 of this Section :

(l) breaking down of material necessary to comply with the requirements of fill ;

(m) waiting for frozen unsuitable material to thaw ;

(n) haulage, deposition in temporary stock piles including the provision of sites for stockpiles.

5 Insert the following paragraph 17(A)

17(A) Deposition of fill in landscape areas and noise barrier earth mounds shall be measured in accordance with paragraph 67 hereof.

6 Insert the following as paragraph 22(A)

22(A) Notwithstanding the provisions of paragraph 22 of this Section the measurement of disposal of suitable material shall, where suitable material is deposited in landscape areas and noise barrier earth mounds, be the volume calculated in accordance with that paragraph, less the volume of compacted suitable fill material calculated in accordance with paragraph 71 hereof.

7 Insert the following as paragraph 23(A)

23(A) Notwithstanding the provisions of paragraph 23 of this Section, the measurement of disposal of unsuitable material shall, where unsuitable material is deposited in landscape areas and noise barrier earth mounds, be the volume calculated in accordance with that paragraph less the volume of compacted unsuitable fill material calculated in accordance with paragraph 71 hereof.

8 Insert the following as paragraph 35(A)

35(A) The compaction of fill in landscape areas and noise barrier earth mounds shall be measured in accordance with paragraph 71 hereof.

9 Insert the following additional paragraphs number 66 to 73 inclusive

Units

Landscape Areas and Noise Barrier Earth Mounds
Deposition of Fill

66 The units of measurement shall be :

(i) deposition of fill . . . . cubic metre.

**Measurement of
Deposition of Fill
in landscape Areas and
Noise Barrier Earth
Mounds**

67 Deposition of fill shall be measured separately for each of the Group III features. The measurement shall be the volume of the compacted fill, calculated in accordance with paragraph 71.

Itemisation

68 Separate items shall be provided for deposition of fill in accordance with Part II paragraphs **3** and **4** and the following:

Group	Feature
I	1 Deposition.
II	1 Suitable material. 2 Unsuitable material.
III	1 In landscape area. 2 In noise barrier earth mounds.

**Deposition of Fill
in Landscape Areas
and Noise Barrier
Earth Mounds
Item coverage**

69 The items for deposition of fill in landscape areas and noise barrier earth mounds shall in accordance with the Preambles to Bill of Quantities General Directions include for:

(*a*) *haulage;*

(*b*) *selection of material of stated types and layering or depositing in locations indicated on Drawings;*

(*c*) *the mechanical or chemical treatment of soil as the Contractor may require to facilitate the use of particular plant;*

(*d*) *complying with requirements for the sequence or rate of deposition;*

(*e*) *depositing fill to slope away from vertical drainage layers and providing temporary drainage to prevent surface water from entering such drainage layers;*

(*f*) *multiple handling of excavated material;*

(*g*) *keeping earthworks free of water;*

(*h*) *waiting for frozen material to thaw;*

(*i*) *trimming and shaping to required levels and contours;*

(*j*) *taking precautions to avoid damage to property, structures, sewers, drains and services;*

(*k*) *replacing suitable material rendered unsuitable;*

(*l*) *deposition of fill resulting from settlement or penetration.*

Compaction of Fill

Units
70 The units of measurement shall be:
   (i) compaction.....................cubic metre

Measurement of Compaction of Fill in Landscape Areas and Noise Barrier Earth Mounds
71 The measurement of compaction of fill:
   (a) In landscape areas;
   (b) In noise barrier earth mounds,
shall be the volume of the void filled to the outline shown on the Drawings or ordered by the Engineer.

Itemisation
72 Separate items shall be provided for compaction of fill in accordance with Part II paragraphs 3 and 4 and the following:

Group	Feature
I	1 Compaction of suitable fill material.
	2 Compaction of unsuitable fill material.
II	1 In landscape area.
	2 In noise barrier earth mounds.

Compaction of Fill in Landscape Areas as Noise Barrier Earth Mounds Item coverage
73 *The items for compaction of fill in landscape areas and noise barrier earth mounds shall in accordance with the Preambles to Bill of Quantities General Directions include for:*

(a) *spreading and levelling;*
(b) *keeping the earthworks free of water;*
(c) *forming and trimming of side slopes, benchings and berms;*
(d) *taking precautions to avoid damage to property, structures, sewers, drains and services;*
(e) *complying with requirements for the sequence or rate of filling;*
(f) *compaction of fill resulting from settlement or penetration.*

Gabion Walling and Mattresses

Units
74 The units of measurement shall be:
   (i) gabion walling, mattresses..........cubic metres...

Measurement
75 The measurement of gabion walling and mattresses shall be the volume contained within the outline of the gabions or mattresses shown on the Drawings or ordered by the Engineer.

Itemisation
76 Separate items shall be provided for gabion walling and mattresses in accordance with Part II paragraphs 3 and 4 and the following:

Group	Feature
I	1 Gabion walling.
	2 Mattresses.

II	1 Different mesh materials.
III	1 Different mesh size.
IV	1 Different types of fill.
V	1 Mattresses installed at 10° or less to the horizontal. 2 Mattresses installed at more than 10° to the horizontal.

Gabion Walling and Mattresses

Item coverage

77 The items for gabion walling and mattresses shall in accordance with the Preambles to Bill of Quantities General Directions include for:
(a) levelling and preparation;
(b) assembling, placing and tying together in position;
(c) staking and tensioning;
(d) cutting and folding mesh to form special units and shapes;
(e) filling with specified fill material including overfilling to allow for settlement;
(f) bracing wires and wiring lids after filling;
(g) special filling where specified to form fair faced finish;
(h) in the case of watercourses, working in and dealing with the flow of water.

Item	Root Narratives	Unit
	Landscape Areas and Noise Barrier Earth Mounds **Deposition of Fill**	
1	Deposition of *A* in *B*.	cu m
	Compaction of Fill	
2	Compaction of *A* in *B*.	cu m
	Gabion Walling and Mattresses	
3	Gabion walling comprising *C* steel wire mesh nominal size *D* with *F* fitting.	cu m
4	Mattress comprising *C* steel wire mesh nominal size *D* with *F* filling installed *E*.	cu m

Group	Variables		
A	*1*	=	suitable material
	2	=	unsuitable material
B	*1*	=	landscape areas
	2	=	noise barrier earth mounds

Group	Variables		
C	1	=	galvanised
	2	=	PVC coated
D	1	=	60 mm × 80 mm
	2	=	50 mm × 70 mm
	3	=	100 mm × 120 mm
E	1	=	at 10° or less to the horizontal
	2	=	at more than 10° to the horizontal
F	1 etc =		[Engineers reference for type of filling]

Section 8: Sub-base and Roadbase

Units

Continuously Reinforced Concrete Roadbase

1 The units of measurement shall be:

(i) continuously reinforced concrete roadbase

.................square metre.

Measurement

2 The measurement of roadbase whether laid in one or more layers shall be calculated using the outlines shown on the Drawings, or ordered by the Engineer, including any projection into the verge or central reserve, and shall be described as in carriageway or hard shoulder as appropriate.

Where carriageway roadbase projects into the hard shoulder and is of a differing thickness to the roadbase in that hard shoulder, then the projection shall be measured with and described as roadbase in carriageway.

The roadbase in hard strip shall be measured with and described as roadbase in carriageway.

Trial lengths will be measured only if they are accepted as part of the Permanent Works.

3 No deduction shall be made for openings of 1 square metre or less.

Itemisation

4 Separate items shall be provided for continuously reinforced concrete roadbase in accordance with Part II paragraphs 3 and 4 and the following:

Group	Feature
I	1 Each type of continuously reinforced concrete roadbase.
II	1 In carriageway. 2 In hard shoulder.
III	1 Different thicknesses.

Continuously Reinforced Concrete Roadbase

Item coverage

5 *The items for continuously reinforced concrete roadbase shall in accordance with the Preambles to Bill of Quantities General Directions include for:*

(a) concrete carriageway and concrete hard shoulder (as Section 10 paragraph 6).

Item	Root Narratives	Unit
1	**Continuously Reinforced Concrete Roadbase** Type *A* continuously reinforced concrete roadbase *B* thick *C*.	sq m

Group	Variables		
A	*1* etc =	[Engineers type reference]	
B	*1*	=	130 mm
	2	=	140 mm
	3	=	150 mm
	4	=	160 mm
	5	=	170 mm
	6	=	180 mm
	7	=	190 mm
	8	=	200 mm
	9	=	220 mm
	10	=	230 mm
	11	=	240 mm
	12	=	250 mm
	13	=	260 mm
	14	=	270 mm
	15	=	280 mm
	16	=	290 mm
C	*1*	=	in carriageway
	2	=	in hard shoulder

Section 9: Flexible Surfacing

Scarifying, Planning, or Burning off Flexible Pavements

Notes

1 The removal of existing flexible pavements by scarifying, planing or burning off should only be measured where these operations are required in connection with re-surfacing or regrading. Where such operations are carried out as a first stage to further excavation they should be measured as Earthworks.

Units

Scarifying, Planing or Burning off Flexible Pavements
1 The units of measurement shall be:
    (i) scarifying flexible pavements, planing or burning off flexible pavements...............square metre.

Itemisation

2 Separate items shall be provided for scarifying, planing or burning off flexible pavements in accordance with Part II paragraphs 3 and 4 and the following:

Group	Feature
I	1 Scarifying flexible pavements. 2 Planing or burning off flexible pavements.
II	1 Different depths.

Scarifying Flexible Pavements, Planing or Burning off Flexible Pavements
Item coverage

3 *The items for scarifying flexible pavements, planing or burning off flexible pavements shall in accordance with the Preambles to Bill of Quantities General Directions include for:*

(a) re-shaping and rolling;
(b) shaping to cambers, falls and crowns;
(c) breakdown of material to comply with the requirements of fill;
(d) multiple handling of material;
(e) disposal of surplus material.

Item	Root Narratives	Unit
	Scarifying, Planing or Burning off Flexible Pavements	
1	*A* flexible pavements not exceeding *B* depth.	sq m

Group	Variables		
A	*1*	=	Scarifying
	2	=	Planing or burning off
B	*1* etc =		[depth as required]

Section 11: Kerbs and Footways

Additional Concrete for Kerbing Channelling and Edging

Notes

1 Additional concrete for kerbing, channelling and edging should only be measured where the Engineer has ordered concrete in excess of the standard foundation details shown on the Drawings.

Footways and Paved Areas

2 Bill items for footways and paved areas should be for the complete construction. In cases where an Engineers Group reference is specified for the whole construction, the total thickness of the combined sub-base, basecourse, wearing course and/or surface dressing or slab should be stated. In all other cases, the individual thicknesses of the respective courses should be stated.

Where the Engineer permits alternative materials, these should be scheduled on the Drawings and cross referenced to the bill item by a Group letter or number.

Remove from Store and Relay Kerbing Channelling, Edging and Paving

3 Full details of foundations required for the relaying of kerbing, channelling, edging and paving should be shown on the Drawings.

Additional Concrete for Kerbing, Channelling and Edging

Units

1 The units of measurement shall be:
 (i) additional concrete...............cubic metre.

Measurement

2 The measurement of additional concrete shall be the volume shown on the Drawing or ordered by the Engineer in excess of the standard requirements shown in the Contract for each type of kerbing, channelling or edging.

Itemisation

3 Separate items shall be provided for additional concrete for kerbing, channelling and edging in accordance with Part II paragraphs 3 and 4 and the following:

Group	Feature
I	1 Additional concrete.
II	1 Kerbing. 2 Channelling. 3 Edging.

III 1 Straight or curved over 12 metres radius.
2 Curves of 12 metres radius or less.

Additional Concrete

Item coverage

4 *The items for additional concrete shall in accordance with the Preambles to Bill of Quantities General Directions include for:*
(a) *excavation and loading into transport, upholding the sides and keeping the earthworks free of water;*
(b) *formwork (as Section 14 paragraph 4);*
(c) *reinforcement (as Section 15 paragraph 5);*
(d) *in situ concrete (as Section 16 paragraph 4);*
(e) *making, filling and sealing joints;*
(f) *surface finishing, curing and protecting;*
(g) *drainage holes or pipes through concrete;*
(h) *disposal of surplus material.*

Footways

Units

5 The units of measurements shall be:
(i) footways..................square metre.

Measurement

6 The measurement of footways shall be calculated using the width of the top surface of the footway.
No deduction shall be made for openings of 1 square metre or less.

Itemisation

7 Separate items shall be provided for footways in accordance with Part II paragraphs 3 and 4 and the following:

Group	Feature
I	1 Footways.
II	1 Flexible construction. 2 Rigid construction.
III	1 Different thicknesses.
IV	1 Different groups or types.
V	1 Different thicknesses of sub-base.

Footways

Item coverage

8 *The items for footways shall in accordance with the Preambles to Bill of Quantities General Directions include for:*
(a) *sub-base (as Section 8 paragraph 7);*
(b) *flexible surfacing (as Section 9 paragraph 9);*
(c) *concrete carriageway (as Section 10 paragraph 6).*

Units

Paved Areas
9 The units of measurement shall be :
   (i) paved areas.................square metre.

Measurement

10 The measurement of paved areas shall be calculated using the width of the top surface of the paving.
No deduction shall be made for openings of 1 square metre or less.

Itemisation

11 Separate items shall be provided for paved areas in accordance with Part II paragraphs 3 and 4 and the following :

Group	Feature
I	1 Paved areas.
II	1 Flexible construction.
	2 Rigid construction.
	3 Flag construction.
III	1 Different thicknesses.
IV	1 Different groups or types.
V	1 Different thicknesses of sub-base.
VI	1 Surfaces sloping at 10° or less to the horizontal.
	2 Surfaces sloping at more than 10° to the horizontal.

Paved Areas

Item coverage

12 *The items for paved areas shall in accordance with the Preambles to Bill of Quantities General Directions include for:*
(a) sub-base (as Section 8 paragraph 7);
(b) flexible surfacing (as Section 9 paragraph 9);
(c) concrete carriageway (as Section 10 paragraph 6);
(d) concrete paved footways (as Section 11 paragraph 13).

Units

Remove from Store and Relay
Kerbing, Channelling and Edging
13 The units of measurement shall be :
   (i) remove from store and relay........linear metre.....

Measurement

14 The measurement of remove from store and relay kerbing, channelling and edging shall be the length of the work.
No deduction shall be made for gaps of 1 linear metre or less.

Itemisation

15 Separate items shall be provided for remove from store and relay kerbing, channelling and edging in accordance with Part II paragraphs 3 and 4 and the following :

Group	Feature
I	1 Remove from store and relay.
II	1 Kerbing. 2 Channelling. 3 Edging.
III	1 Different materials and designs.
IV	1 Straight or curved over 12 metres radius. 2 Curves of 12 metres radius or less.

Remove from Store and Relay

Item coverage

16 *The items for remove from store and relay shall in accordance with the Preambles to Bill of Quantities General Directions include for:*
(a) *collecting from Contractor's store;*
(b) *replacing items damaged during storage;*
(c) *kerbing, channelling and edging (as Section 11 paragraph 4).*

**Remove from Store and Relay
Paving**

Units

17 The unit of measurement shall be:
(i) remove from store and relay........square metre.

Measurement

18 The measurement of remove from store and relay paving shall be calculated using the width of the top surface of the paving.
No deduction shall be made for openings of 1 square metre or less.

Itemisation

19 Separate items shall be provided for remove from store and relay paving in accordance with Part II paragraphs 3 and 4 and the following:

Group	Feature
I	1 Remove from store and relay.
II	1 Paving in footways. 2 Paving in paved areas.
III	1 Different types.
IV	1 Different thicknesses.
V	1 Different thicknesses of sub-base.

VI 1 Paved area surfaces sloping at 10° or
less to the horizontal.
2 Paved area surfaces sloping at more than
10° to the horizontal.

**Remove from Store
and Relay**

Item coverage

20 *The items for remove from store and relay shall in accordance with the Preambles to Bill of Quantities General
Directions include for:*
(a) *collecting from Contractor's store;*
(b) *replacing items damaged during storage;*
(c) *concrete paved footways (as Section 11 paragraph 13).*

Item	Root Narratives	Unit
	Additional Concrete for Kerbing, Channelling and Edging	
1	Additional concrete for **AB**.	cu m
	Footways	
2	Flexible constructed footway permitted alternative materials **CD** thick in total as Drawing No **J**.	sq m
3	Flexible constructed footway comprising of **E** sub-base **D** thick **GD** thick **HD** thick **I**.	sq m
4	**D** concrete footway on **E** sub-base **D** thick.	sq m
	Paved areas	
5	Flexible constructed paved area permitted alternative materials **CD** thick in total as Drawing No **J** to **F**.	sq m
6	Flexible constructed paved area comprising of **E** sub-base **D** thick **GD** thick **HD** thick **I** to **F**.	sq m
7	**D** concrete paved area on **E** sub-base **D** thick to **F**.	sq m
8	**K** precast concrete paving flags in paved area on **E** sub-base **D** thick to **F**.	sq m
9	**LM** in paved area on **E** sub-base **D** thick to **F**.	sq m
	Remove from Store and Relay **Kerbing, Channelling and Edging**	
10	Remove from store and relay **NAOB**.	lin m
	Remove from Store and Relay Paving	
11	Remove from store and relay **K** precast concrete paving flags in footways on **E** sub-base **D** thick.	sq m
12	Remove from store and relay **LM** in footways on **E** sub-base **D** thick.	sq m

Item	Root Narratives	Unit
13	Remove from store and relay **K** precast concrete paving flags in paved areas on **E** sub-base **D** thick to **F**.	sq m
14	Remove from store and relay **LM** in paved areas on **E** sub-base **D** thick to **F**.	sq m

Group	Variables		
A	**1**	=	kerbing
	2	=	channelling
	3	=	edging
B	**1**	=	straight or curved over 12 metres radius
	2	=	curves of 12 metres radius or less
C	**1** etc =		[Engineers Group reference]
D	**0**	=	No entry
	1 etc =		[thickness as required]
E	**0**	=	No entry
	1	=	Group A
	2	=	Group B
	3	=	Group C
	4	=	Granular Type 1
	5	=	Granular Type 2
	6	=	Soil Cement
	7	=	Cement bound granular
	8	=	Lean concrete
	9	=	Wet lean concrete
F	**1**	=	surface sloping at 10° or less to the horizontal
	2	=	surfaces sloping at more than 10° to the horizontal
G	**0**	=	No entry
	1	=	rolled asphalt basecourse
	2	=	dense bitumen macadam basecourse
	3	=	dense tarmacadam basecourse
	4	=	bitumen macadam basecourse
	5	=	tarmacadam basecourse
	6	=	[Engineers Group reference]
H	**0**	=	No entry
	1	=	rolled asphalt wearing course
	2	=	dense bitumen macadam wearing course
	3	=	cold asphalt wearing course

Group	Variables		
H *contd.*	**4**	=	open textured bitumen macadam wearing course
	5	=	tarmacadam wearing course
	6	=	single course mastic asphalt
	7	=	[Engineers Group reference]
I	**0**	=	No entry
	1 etc =		and surface dressing [Engineers specification and thickness]
J	**1** etc =		[Engineers Drawing number reference]
K	**1**	=	600 mm × 450 mm × 50 mm thick
	2	=	600 mm × 600 mm × 50 mm thick
	3	=	600 mm × 750 mm × 50 mm thick
	4	=	600 mm × 900 mm × 50 mm thick
L	**1** etc =		[Engineers specification and size]
M	**1**	=	stone paving flags
	2	=	block paving
	3	=	cobble paving
	4	=	brick paving
	5	=	granite sett paving
	6 etc =		[other named material]
N	**1**	=	precast concrete
	2	=	stone
	3	=	granite
O	**1** etc =		[Engineers type design]

Section 12: Traffic Signs and Road Markings

	Notes
Remove from Store and Re-erect Traffic Signs	**1** Full details of foundations required for the re-erection of traffic signs should be shown on the Drawings.

Remove from Store and Re-erect Traffic Signs

Unit	**1** The units of measurement shall be: (i) remove from store and re-erect traffic signs..................number.
Measurement	**2** The measurement of remove from store and re-erect traffic signs shall be the complete installation.
Itemisation	**3** Separate items shall be provided for remove from store and re-erect traffic signs in accordance with Part II paragraphs 3 and 4 and the following:

Group	Feature
I	1 Remove from store and re-erect traffic signs.
II	1 Different types.

Remove from Store and Re-erect Traffic Signs Item coverage

4 *The items for remove from store and re-erect traffic signs shall in accordance with the Preambles to Bill of Quantities General Directions include for:*
(a) collecting from Contractor's store;
(b) replacing items damaged during storage;
(c) traffic signs (as Section 12 paragraph 4).

Item	Root Narratives	Unit
	Remove from Store and Re-erect Traffic Signs	
1	Remove from store and re-ect **AB**.	No

Group	Variables		
A	*1*	=	traffic sign
	2	=	traffic sign including posts
	3	=	internally illuminated traffic sign
	4	=	internally illuminated traffic sign including posts
	5	=	externally illuminated traffic sign
	6	=	externally illuminated traffic sign including posts
B	**1** etc =		[Engineers reference]

Printed in England for Her Majesty's Stationery Office by Tonbridge Printers Ltd, Tonbridge. Kent
Dd 587291 K56 11/77